A Straight Talking Introduction to

Caring for Someone with Mental Health Problems

Jen Kilyon
&
Theresa Smith

PCCS BOOKS
Ross-on-Wye

First published in 2009

PCCS BOOKS Ltd
2 Cropper Row
Alton Road
Ross-on-Wye
Herefordshire
HR9 5LA
UK
Tel +44 (0)1989 763900
www.pccs-books.co.uk

**A Straight Talking Introduction to
Caring for Someone with Mental Health Problems**

A CIP catalogue record for this book is available from the British Library

ISBN 978 1 906254 18 6

Cover designed in the UK by Old Dog Graphics
Typeset in the UK by The Old Dog's Missus
Printed in the UK by Ashford Colour Press, Gosport, Hampshire

Contents

Series introduction   v
Richard Bentall and Pete Sanders

Introduction to this book   1
Jen Kilyon and Theresa Smith

1   Institutionalised madness   9
Liz Swannack

2   Loving Christian   27
Georgina Wakefield

3   Neglect and abuse   39
Morgan Winterburn

4   Memories, medication and meaning in   53
manufacturing madness
Marion Hughes

5   A young carer: Jasmeen's story   72
Jasmeen

6   Is anyone there? Will someone please   77
listen? More questions than answers
Anne Fraser

7   Emergent themes and suggestions for   92
improving care
Jen Kilyon and Theresa Smith

Appendix 1: Helpful learning and information   114
distilled from carers' experiences

Appendix 2: Resources   119

Index   132

Note: Fictitious names have been used to protect the anonymity of those appearing in this book, except in Chapter 2.

Acknowledgements

We would like to thank the following people: Phil Thomas for first suggesting we become involved in this project. Peter Relton, Judith Varley and Patricia Chambers for their advice. Drew Lindon at the Princess Royal Trust for Carers. Maureen Jackson for believing in us and for keeping us going through the long hard years.

Our friends and family who have supported us – they know who they are.

All the friends, carers and family members we've met along the way who have inspired us with their fortitude, determination and, against the odds, their good humour.

And finally, Pete Sanders and the editorial team at PCCS Books for their patience, encouragement and well-placed advice.

Abbreviations

CAMHS	Child and Adolescent Mental Health Services
CCTA	Creating Capable Teams Approach
CMHS	Community Mental Health Service
CMHT	Community Mental Health Team
CPA	Care Programme Approach
CPN	Community Psychiatric Nurse
EIP	Early Intervention in Psychosis
HEE	High Expressed Emotion
IAPT	Increased Access to Psychological Therapies
MHA	Mental Health Act
MHAC	Mental Health Act Commission
NHS	National Health Service
NIMHE	National Institute for Mental Health in England
PALS	Patient Advice and Liaison Service
PICU	Psychiatric Intensive Care Unit
PRN	Pro re nata – as needed
RMO	Responsible Medical Officer
SCT	Supervised Community Treatment
STR	Support, Time and Recovery
TRS	Treatment Resistant Schizophrenia

Introduction to the *Straight Talking* series

What are mental health problems?

Much of what is written and spoken about emotional distress or mental health problems implies that they are illnesses. This can lead us all too easily to believe that we no longer have to think about mental health problems, because illness is best left to doctors. They are the illness experts, and psychiatrists are the doctors who specialise in mental illness. This series of books is different because we don't think that all mental health problems should be automatically regarded as illnesses.

If mental health problems aren't necessarily illnesses, it means that the burden of responsibility for distress in our lives should not be entirely shouldered by doctors and psychiatrists. All citizens have a responsibility, however small, in creating a world where everyone has a decent opportunity to live a fulfilling life. This is a contentious idea, but one which we want to advance alongside the dominant medical view.

Rather than accept that solutions to mental health problems are 'owned' by the medical profession, we will take a good look at alternatives which involve the users of psychiatric services, their carers, families, friends and other 'ordinary people' taking control of their own lives. One of the tools required in order to become active in mental health issues, whether your own or other people's, is knowledge. This series of books is a starting point for anyone who wants to know more about mental health.

How these books are written

We want these books to be understandable, so we use everyday language wherever possible. The books could have been almost completely jargon-free, but we thought that including some technical and medical terms would be helpful. Most doctors, psychiatrists and psychologists use the medical model of mental illness and manuals to help them diagnose mental health problems. The medical model and the diagnostic manuals use a particular set of terms to describe what doctors think of as 'conditions'. Although these words aren't very good at describing individual people's experiences, they are used a lot in psychiatric and psychological services, so we thought it would be helpful to define these terms as we went along and use them in a way that might help readers understand what the professionals mean. We don't expect that psychiatrists and psychologists and others working in mental health services will stop using medical terminology (although we think it might be respectful for them to drop it when talking to their patients and their families), so these books should help you get used to, and learn *their* language.

The books also contain resources for further learning in the appendices (pp. 114ff). As well as lists of books, websites and organisations at the end of the book, there are endnotes. These will not be important to everyone, but they do tell the reader where information – a claim about effectiveness, an argument for or against, or a quotation – has come from so you can follow it up if you wish.

Being realistic and reassuring

Our aim is to be realistic – neither overly optimistic nor pessimistic. Things are nearly always more complicated than we would like them to be. Honest evaluations of mental health problems, of what might cause them, of what can help, and of what the likely outcome might be, are, like so much in life, somewhere in between. For the vast majority of people it would be wrong to say that they have an illness from which they will never recover. But it would be equally wrong to say that they will be completely unchanged by the distressing thoughts and feelings they are having. Life is an accumulation of experiences. There is usually no pill, or any other treatment for that matter, that will take us back to 'how we were before'. There are many things we can do (and we will be looking at lots of them in this series) in collaboration with doctors, psychiatrists, psychologists, counsellors, indeed everyone working in mental health services, with the help of our friends and family, or on our own, which stand a good chance of helping us feel better and build a constructive life with hope for the future.

Of course, we understand that the experiences dealt with in these books can sometimes be so overwhelming, confusing and terrifying that people will try to escape from them by withdrawing, going mad or even by trying to kill themselves. This happens when our usual coping strategies fail us. We accept that killing oneself is, in some circumstances, a rational act – that for the person in question it can make a lot of sense. Nonetheless, we believe that much of the distress that underpins such an extreme course of action, from which there can be no turning back, is avoidable. For this reason, all of the books in this series point towards realistic hope and recovery.

Debates

There is no single convenient answer to many of the most important questions explored in these books. No matter how badly we might wish for a simple answer, what we have is a series of debates, or arguments more like, between stakeholders and there are many stakeholders whose voices demand space in these books. We use the word 'stakeholders' here because service users, carers, friends, family, doctors, psychologists, psychiatrists, nurses and other workers, scientists in drug companies, therapists, indeed all citizens, have a stake in how our society understands and deals with problems of mental health. It is simultaneously big business and intimately personal, and many things in between. As we go along, we try to explain how someone's stake in distress (including our own, where we can see it), whether business or personal, can influence their experience and judgement.

Whilst we want to present competing (sometimes opposing) viewpoints, we don't want to leave the reader high and dry to evaluate complicated debates on their own. We will try to present reasonable conclusions which might point in certain directions for personal action. Above all, though, we believe that knowledge is power and that the better informed you are, even though the information might be conflicting, the more able you will be to make sound decisions.

It's also useful to be reminded that the professionals involved in helping distressed people are themselves caught in the same flow of conflicting information. It is their *job*, however, to interpret it in our service, so that the best solutions are available to as many people as possible. You may have noticed that the word 'best' brings with it certain challenges, not least of all, what we mean when we use this term. Perhaps the best means the most effective? However, even using words like 'effective' doesn't completely clear up the puzzle. An effective treatment could be the one which returns someone to work quickly, if you are an employer, or one which makes someone feel happier and more calm, if they are your son or daughter. Readers will also know from recent press coverage that the National Institute for Health and Clinical Excellence (NICE) which evaluates and recommends treatments, keeps one eye on the budget, so 'effective' might mean 'cost effective' to some people. This brings us to evidence.

Evidence

Throughout these books there will be material which we will present as 'evidence'. This is one of the most contentious terms to be found in this series. One person's evidence is another person's fanciful mythology and yet another person's oppressive propaganda. Nevertheless the term crops up increasingly in everyday settings, most relevantly when we hear of 'evidence-based practice'. The idea behind this term is that the treatments psychologists and psychiatrists offer should be those that work. Crudely put, there should be some evidence that, say, talking about problems, or taking a prescribed drug, actually helps people to feel better. We encounter a real problem however, when trying to evaluate this evidence, as the books will demonstrate. We will try not to discount any 'evidence' out of hand, but we will evaluate it, and we will do this with a bias towards scientific evaluation.

The types of evidence that will be covered in these books, along with their positive and negative points, include the following.

Research methods, numbers and statistics

On the one hand, the logic of most research is simple, but on the other hand, the way things have to be arranged to avoid bias in the results can lead to a perplexing system of measurements. Even the experts lose the sense of it sometimes. We'll try to explain the logic of studies, but almost certainly leave out the details. You can look these up yourself if you wish.

The books in this series look at research into a wide range of issues regarding mental health problems, including the experience of distress, what is known about the causes of problems, and their prevention and treatment. Different research methods are more or less appropriate for each of these areas, so we will be looking at different types of research as we go along. We say this now because many readers may be most familiar with studies into the *effective treatments* of distress, and we want to emphasise that there are many credible and valid sources of essential information about distress that are sometimes overlooked.

You may have come across the idea that some research methods are 'better' than others – that they constitute a 'gold standard'. In the case of research into the effectiveness of different treatments, the gold standard is usually considered to be 'randomised controlled trials' (RCTs). In simple terms, RCTs are complex (and often very expensive) experiments in which a group of individuals who all suffer from the same problem are randomly allocated to a treatment or a 'control' condition (at its simplest, no treatment at all) to see whether the treatment works. We are not necessarily convinced that RCTs always *are* the best way of conducting research into effective treatments, but they are, at the present time, the method given most credence by bodies which control funding, such as the National Health Service's National Institute of Health and Clinical Excellence (NICE), so we need to understand them.

Personal experience

Personal experience is an important source of evidence to the extent that nowadays, people who have suffered debilitating psychiatric distress are sometimes called 'experts by experience'. Personal stories provide an essential counterbalance to the impersonal numbers and statistics often found in research projects such as RCTs. Whilst not everyone is average, by definition, most people are. Balancing the average results obtained from RCTs with some personal stories helps complete the picture and is now widely accepted to the extent that it has given birth to the new field of 'survivor research'.

Understanding contexts

Widening our view to include the families and lives of people, and the cultural, economic, social and political settings in which we live completes the picture. Mental health problems are connected to the conditions in which we all live, just as much as they are connected to our biology. From the start we want readers to know that, if there is one message or model which the books are trying to get across, it is that problems in mental health are more often than not the result of complex events in the environments in which we live and our reactions to them. These reactions can also be influenced by our biology or the way we have learned to think and feel. Hopefully these books will help disentangle the puzzle of distress and provide positive suggestions and hope for us all, whether we work in the system, currently have mental health problems ourselves, are caring for someone or are friends with someone who has.

We hope that readers of these books will feel empowered by what they learn, and thereby more able to get the best out of mental health services. It would be wonderful if our efforts, directly or indirectly, influence the development of services that effectively address the emotional, social and practical needs of people with mental health problems.

Richard Bentall
Pete Sanders
April 2009

Introduction

Jen Kilyon and Theresa Smith

There are up to 1.5 million people in the UK caring for a relative or friend with a mental health problem.[1]

There are over 50,000 children and young people looking after someone with a mental health problem in the UK.[2]

This means:

1 in 4 carers are mental health carers.

1 in every 40 people is a mental health carer.[3]

This book is intended to be a sharing of experience that might firstly help carers who identify with the contributors and so help validate their own experience or ways forward. Secondly, we hope it will act as a guide for mental health workers to help them understand the reality of caring for a relative with serious mental health difficulties. Thirdly, we

---

1. Page 1 in Briefing Paper *Services to Support Carers of People with Mental Health Problems*. National Co-ordinating Centre for NHS Service Delivery and Organisation (NCCSDO) 2002. This figure include carers looking after people with functional mental health problems as well as dementia.

2. Dearden C & Becker S (2004) *Young Carers in the UK: The 2004 Report*. London: Carers UK and The Children's Society.

3. This figure was derived from two sources: (a) '1 in 6 people will currently be experiencing problems with their mental health' from http://www.shift.org.uk/ aboutus/index.html, accessed 23 May 2007.
(b) UK population at 60,776,238 (July 2007 estimate), from https://www.cia.gov/library/publications/the-world-factbook/print/uk.html, accessed 23 May 2007.

hope it will help organisations wanting to evaluate the ways in which they engage with families, and finally, for those providing education and training who want to include a better understanding of work with families in their curriculum.

For many who find themselves in the caring role, the term 'carer' isn't as straightforward as it might seem. Some carers feel that it unhelpfully 'professionalises' their relationship; others refuse to adopt the title at all. Equally, service users may not recognise those closest to them as their carers. For people in mental turmoil who may be feeling threatened and vulnerable the term can potentially add to greater suspicion, undermine trust and compound the sense for some that their families are working with services against them; it can reduce a service user's sense of autonomy. They may not feel that they need to be 'cared for'.

It can have the effect of denying the relationship that previously existed within the family. It can create a distance both between the family and their relative and between the family and services. When does the role of mother, father, wife, husband, friend or neighbour end and the role of carer begin?[4]

It can also imply that there is only one person who 'cares', whereas in reality, there are a number of people that feature in the life of the person in need who have a contribution to make. The term 'carer' then encompasses a variety of relationships and caring contexts.

Caring about someone in serious mental distress is completely different from caring for someone with a physical condition, as we both know from our own experience of having cared for relatives. Whilst caring for someone who, for

4. NCCSDO (2005) *Positive and Inclusive. Effective ways for professionals to include carers in information sharing.* Report to the National Co-ordinating Centre for NHS | Service Delivery and Organisation, Research & Development.

example, has cancer can be distressing as you watch someone close to you suffer pain and discomfort, if you are at all able to alleviate that discomfort there can be a sense of satisfaction. Similarly fetching and carrying for someone with a broken leg can be wearing but knowing that you are helping the healing process makes it worthwhile. Caring about someone in acute or chronic mental pain brings with it mostly heartache and frustration because there is so little that you can do on your own to take that pain away. A person's inner world cannot be bathed, rubbed, soothed or salved. When that inner world is tormented and tangled with real life experiences and emotions that may be bound up with those closest to them, it makes the role of family members and close friends even more complex. If the person in turmoil has lost touch with reality and cannot communicate what is going on in their mind or distinguish between their confusion and what is actually happening, 'the carer' can unwittingly make situations far worse in their efforts to try and help.

Between us, as a result of our work, we have had the opportunity to meet many people who use services, meeting family members, those working in the front line, middle and senior managers, as well as policy makers and educators at all levels from around the country. Therefore, although there are only a few stories in this book, we know that they represent a much wider picture. We do not discount that there *are* more positive stories than those in this book, and indeed we sought more positive accounts of family experience, but sadly such accounts were not forthcoming.

There are several government schemes, initiatives and action plans which seek to improve and clearly state the services due to carers and users of statutory mental health services. Many of these are detailed in Appendix 2, so that readers will be able to access the right services for themselves or their friends or relatives with mental health problems. There is no doubt that if and when fully and consistently implemented, these charters and initiatives would go a fair way to improving the treatment of service users and enabling the appropriate, respectful involvement of carers. However, the testimony from contributors to this book reveals that provision for people with mental health problems is something of a lottery, as is the attitude shown towards carers. This book simply gives them voice. We might ask if these experiences are representative, yet that could miss an important point. These *are* the genuine experiences of carers and must be accounted for.

Across the country, families are battling with services to receive the best possible treatment for their relative. Why should it be that this battle seems so universal? Evidence from the experiences of contributors and from our wider experience points towards a mental health system that from many carers' points of view is not fit for purpose. Psychiatry in this country is dominated by a medical model which focuses almost exclusively on (i) pharmacology as the primary treatment; (ii) separating the service user from his/her environment and social context; and (iii) reducing him or her to a series of depersonalised symptoms usually taken from the *Diagnostic and Statistical Manual* (*DSM-IV*) – voices, withdrawal, mania, grandiose delusions, hallucinations, grossly disorganised behaviour, disorganised speech, blunted/flat/constricted affect, paranoid ideation, persistent identity disturbance, and so the list goes on. The vocabulary itself is brutal, unyielding and dehumanising.

Using this clinical language as a means by which to describe those with severe mental health problems in effect renders the service user little more than an abstract figure that exists in isolation from their history, family, friends, work, play or community. Therefore those most intimately connected to the person in distress are redundant and they are not required to make any meaningful contribution to the treatment decisions of those they care about and for. These accounts show that family and friends are still not regarded as partners in care as a matter of course alongside the care team, in spite of many studies, guidelines and policies stating how important this is.[5]

Of course we recognise that friendships and familial relationships can be difficult and complicated and that some people with mental health problems will prefer not to have family or friends involved, but this does not preclude the care team from giving both family and, if appropriate, friends and colleagues, the opportunity to contribute their intimate understanding and knowledge of their friend or relative, particularly in their wider social context. It could be said that friends and family are too subjectively involved, or even 'biased'. And in some cases it might even be that some friends and family members are making the situation worse. Whilst this may be so, it shouldn't detract from the fact that families and friends, subjective or not, could have important and significant contributions and observations that might be of use to a care team when considering patient care. Serious mental health problems are not straightforward affairs, it stands to reason therefore that working with families and friends will at times be awkward and tricky, but this is no reason not to try. We know of early intervention in psychosis (EIP) teams, for example, that are working with families as a matter of team policy. But this is not universal.

When friends and family are ignored by statutory services, having no dialogue, sense of inclusion or partnership leaves

---

5. Guidelines and policies from various UK Government and NHS sources, stating the importance of carer support and involvement, are referenced throughout the book and are compiled in Appendix 2.

them peripheral, feeling redundant and can often increase feelings of guilt and blame as they struggle to find meaning and reasons as to why their friend or relative has become so distressed and unwell. They ask themselves, 'Is it something I/we did?' or bemoan 'If only I hadn't done this or that.' Including family – and, where appropriate, friends – and having effective communication with them would enable the sorting of fact from fiction and shed light on where families might have played a part in the mental health problem, and where they are not implicated in the problem. Only when they are appropriately involved can the role of friends and family in the problem be evaluated and addressed.

Absent friends

We have repeatedly referred to 'family and friends' in this introduction, but this conceals at least two omissions.

Firstly, the experiences come exclusively from adult carers – either of their teenage or grown-up children, or their spouse. We have not been able to include any first-person testimony from the army of children who 'care for' a parent or older relative with mental health problems. Here 'care for' covers a huge variety of possibilities, from simply living with, helping with or having to accommodate the complex needs of an older sibling, parent or grandparent in an extended family to being the sole carer of your single-parent mum or dad with a mental health problem. We could not expect writing for this book from a young person, so we have included a short chapter (Chapter 5) which is a distillation and adaptation of the experiences of more than one person. We know that many young carers feel abandoned and desperate, whilst doing their best to live their lives as they look after their mum, dad or other relative.

Secondly, we have no 'active' contribution from a carer from a minority ethnic group. Chapter 5 describes the experiences of a young person of colour, but it is a 'shadow-written' piece based on a couple of real people. Although the names of the contributors, and some demographic details have, in all but one instance, been changed to protect the identities of the people involved, we have not changed the ethnic origins or any of the details which point to the contributors' cultural origins. Apart from the confusion and upset caused by their friend or relative's distressed and distressing behaviour, the experience of being a carer in the UK in the twenty-first century is mainly constructed by the responses, implicit attitudes and actual behaviours of the mental health system and its representatives. The key factor, which seems to overshadow issues of class, gender and other ethnographic factors, is the fact that the carer is perceived as simply that – a carer, and little else. However, we think it is largely the case that a person's skin colour and assumed ethnicity will further configure the responses they are likely to get, and, we fear, not in a positive way. Some issues of ethnicity do arise in Chapter 5.

That there are no voices from black and minority ethnic communities in this book is a cause for concern to us. Whilst to some extent this is down to our own limitations as white, native English speakers, it is also because people from black minority ethnic communities suffer a dual stigma and also because of the thorny issue of integration. People so marginalised and discriminated against are possibly less likely to be active in mental health issues and might feel unable to contribute to books like this.[6] The following factors ameliorate this omission to some extent: (i) we have included a section on resources dedicated to issues regarding black and ethnic minority carers in Appendix 2, and (ii) we strongly believe that the contributors' experiences point to the ways in

6. Of course, there *are* mental health activists from BME communities (see, e.g. Sharing Voices at http://www.sharingvoices.org.uk) and they tend to active *in* those communities.

Joe's suggestion of the Mountains of Mourne sounded much more logical and healing but we didn't know how to wing it.

So Mark had to make one of the most difficult decisions in his life. He had to turn the car around and take Joe back to 'The Mental Home' having reasoned with his son thus: 'Do you trust your parents? Do you believe that we will always do our best for you? Well, we have to go back now and it will work out better in the end for you.' This conversation sits in my soul and I know that it has undermined our relationship with our son. How can he trust us any more when we allowed this to happen? We knew then that it wasn't for the best but were threatened with the law if we'd tried to come up with an alternative.

Within a week Joe deteriorated rapidly. He was smoking cannabis daily and being given ecstasy and cocaine by other patients on the ward. For almost two years at home since Joe had left university we had managed in the main to keep him away from drugs. When I tried to raise this issue with staff they appeared to go into denial that this was a problem. They had put posters up, the jury was still out on the links with cannabis and psychosis, and in any case it was Joe's, not their responsibility. I asked if they had involved the police and was told they had tried but not received any response. I volunteered to help by contacting them myself as I was by now worn down by daily calls from Joe asking me to bring in the £50 he was told he owed to the dealers on the ward, as they were threatening him with violence. The notion that this ward was meant to be a 'therapeutic environment' was laughable. So I called the police drugs team and they were horrified at what I told them. They said they had never received any requests from the hospital. They dealt with the situation thoroughly and professionally, managed to catch the dealers using my tip-offs, gave the management clear messages about what they had found, and ensured that they recognised their responsibilities and duty of care.

I began to feel we might now make some progress. However what I was about to come up against for the first time was the apparent revenge culture of some staff working in mental health services. Joe had mentioned to us that the ward manager had said to him, 'I don't know what your mum and dad are playing at – bringing the police in and getting us into trouble like this.' There was a Mental Health Act Commission (MHAC) tribunal coming up and out of the blue Joe was given unaccompanied leave for the first time on the morning of the tribunal. Now that the police had got rid of the dealers, patients had to find other ways of getting their drugs. Naturally when word got about that someone was 'being let out' they were given a shopping list. So, although he had no money of his own, Joe was given £30 by others on the ward and told exactly what to get and how and where to get it. I find it hard to believe that staff were unaware of this situation because, although the tribunal deemed he was still 'suffering from a mental illness that required his continued detention', early the next morning I got a call from the local police station to ask if Mark or I could come and act as a responsible adult as our son was in a police cell being charged with possession of cannabis. When I called the ward to find out what was going on, I was told, 'That's what happens when you go to the police.' When Mark sat with Joe in the interview room while he was being cautioned, the detective inspector tried to impress upon him the seriousness of what he had done. He stated that it couldn't be a very pleasant experience being held in a police cell overnight and hoped this would be the last time this would happen. Joe's response was that it was actually a blessed relief from being in hospital as at least people treated him kindly and with respect in the police station and that no one shouted at him like they did on the ward.

Joe soon became the archetypal revolving-door patient. In eight months he had three admissions, each time becoming less and less purposeful. When I asked the ward manager if she could see any hope for the future she told me she'd seen all of this so many times before; he was a young lad who needed to face up to his responsibilities and would be back at least another three times before we'd see any progress. I must learn to 'back off and let him live his own life'. I wasn't prepared to just let things drift like this and became involved in service improvements so that I could use our experience to change things, because I knew there must be a better way. This was, to some extent, helpful in that at least I wasn't sitting at home crying and feeling powerless. In this period I did meet some thoughtful committed individuals who wanted to make changes both within and outside statutory services. I learnt much about alternatives to medication and more humane ways of working and began work as a trainer and consultant as well as activist. This was *my* road to recovery, though not always smooth, and there were, and still are, many times when it feels as though I've lost the map and there are no signposts.

Meanwhile Joe continued to be in distress, often putting himself in dangerous situations such as jumping in the canal, walking along telegraph wires, attempting to drive our car over a cliff, and trying to get a lift to London on the platform of an articulated truck about to drive on to the motorway. This led him to being placed, still under Section 3, in the private sector, funded by the NHS at huge expense, in more and more secure places in many different parts of the country. As a skilled rock climber he was always able to escape from these places which he often described as prisons, or 'living on the street'. Rarely were any of them able to provide anything approaching a therapeutic environment. We felt powerless to intervene, since most places appeared to regard us as part of the problem and wanted to keep us at a distance with our difficult questions. We didn't find any examples of organisations within the independent sector with service user or carer representation as part of their governance structures. When we met managers to try to resolve issues, they all appeared to be very defensive and didn't want to have to justify to us their purpose, ethos or environment. It was not our business to ask about staff attitudes and lack of understanding of mental distress and how to work psychologically. Their communication policies, management strategy and mechanisms for governance and accountability were nothing to do with us and apparently of little interest to the local NHS commissioners who were shelling out a fortune for CRAP (not, in my experience, Commission Reviewed Assessment Process). Time after time we came across the same scenario, that if we attempted to make a complaint about some of the appalling practices we came across, there were difficult consequences for ourselves and Joe.

Things had now got so bad that no one appeared to know what to do. Six years had elapsed and Joe had been detained under Section 3 of the MHA for most of that time. He was in his twelfth institution – most of them in the private sector where they claimed to be able to work with people who have complex needs. All appeared to have given up on him after having tried massive doses of drugs in a whole range of combinations – polypharmacy writ large. In some places there may have been one individual member of staff who could connect with Joe but this was useless against a tide of ignorance of psychological factors such as trauma-induced psychosis.

Joe was becoming increasingly angry with us – no doubt blaming us as the people he thought had some power to change things yet all we appeared to be doing was allowing him to end up in worse and worse places. He frequently referred to situations from the past where he had obviously been having a difficult time in response to a whole series of things that had happened to him. I was the main target of his anger and distress. Why did I hate him? How had I allowed people to lock him up? Why did I go around helping others and abandon him? When we tried to organise leave for him there would often be incidents – possibly some self-sabotage going on – where Joe either ran away or did very risky things. This resulted in most staff becoming extremely risk averse and refusing to take him out of the building. It meant that most days the only bit of fresh air he experienced was ten minutes every hour inside a cage, referred to by the staff as a 'courtyard', surrounded by walls, without a blade of grass, a leaf or a tree in sight. Joe told us it was hard 'living on the street' and I can imagine that being stuck on a corridor with 14 other angry distressed young men must have, to him, seemed akin to that experience. What were we to do? We could see no hope on the horizon.

The community team had some exceptional staff, one who connected very well with Joe – no doubt because of his own personal experiences that I suspect may have mirrored some of the distress that had happened to Joe before he became tangled in the psychiatric system. He knew that unless and until we were able to help Joe deal with the difficulties that led to his psychosis, no combination of drugs coupled with incarceration was going to make any lasting difference and was in fact causing untold harm. We tried suggesting to the Responsible Medical Officer (RMO) that we needed to work psychologically but were told this would not be a good idea as it 'may open a Pandora's box'. My response was to remind him that the last thing to come out of the fabled box was hope and that without this we all struggle to survive. It was therefore eventually decided to begin doing some family work on the ward with one particular member of staff who had empathy for us and could understand Joe and support him after each session. We then started to see some progress. At last Joe began to try and make sense of things from the past that had been troubling him for years. We knew this wasn't going to be easy. It would take a long time to undo the damage that the original distresses and the subsequent misdiagnosis and ill-treatment had done.

A few staff understood that their role was to support Joe through this process, not put too many demands on him, and to help manage any fallout there may be. One exceptional nurse even went out of her way to ensure Joe had a birthday to remember in the middle of this traumatic time. Sadly some staff didn't want or like what was going on, as they only saw more problems for themselves with a young man, at times confused and angry. He was having to see things from the past in a different light. He may have been struggling to take some responsibility for some life events and begin to shed guilt and deal with grief for others where he had no control. I know this was leading to more difficult psychotic periods as Joe was trying to work through deeply held experiences and some staff were reacting adversely to this, blaming us for allowing him to stay there, when according to them he was 'inappropriately placed'. I know that some staff just wanted the drugs to be increased to make the situation more manageable for them in the short term. We had noticed that the PRN[1] medication was already being used with an alarming degree of frequency. One nurse in particular told me my son had complex needs and this was a rehab (rehabilitation) ward so why was I preventing him being sent to a more secure place. This was in spite of the fact that the ward was advertised for people with complex needs.

---

1. Pro re nata – medicine to be taken as necessary.

She said that my son was far too ill to be there and that plenty of places had been suggested where he could go and it was my fault he wasn't receiving the complex care he needed. She blamed Joe for the three attacks there had been on him on this ward, accusing him of having provoked them (it had been made clear to us by the ward manager that this was certainly not the case) and furthermore, that the way he was behaving was going to lead to him being beaten up again, and that I was the real root of the problem.

We believed that some staff, and this nurse in particular, were trying to crank the situation up so that Joe's condition and responses to more distress would escalate so that he would have 'to be disposed of'. That was the exact language this nurse had used with us previously in relation to another client to try and persuade us to press charges against this other client on one of the occasions when Joe had been attacked by him on the ward. When we realised what was happening and complained about this member of staff, the repercussions for us all were horrendous.

Two days after we went to talk to the ward manager about this situation, when she had acknowledged that the nurse had acted unprofessionally, we discovered that because a report had been made by a member of the ward staff, a series of major events took place which had very serious consequences for us all. This prevented the person who Joe most trusted from working with him for a long time. It also meant that the family work couldn't continue. I believe Joe was left very distressed with a lot of issues unresolved, feeling frightened, angry and guilty. His response, as on many previous occasions, was to try to run away. He managed to scale a very high security fence but was brought back straight away. When, the following evening, he tried to make another exit by breaking the tiles on his bedroom ceiling and attempting to climb into the space above, he was transferred to the local NHS Psychiatric Intensive Care

Unit (PICU) which had just opened.

We temporarily breathed a sigh of relief, imagining that once Joe was back within the NHS it would be much easier for the home team to liaise and for us to be more actively and positively involved in his care. We thought that as this was a brand new unit for people who didn't respond well to being on an acute ward, the staff would have been selected for their expertise in dealing with complex cases and we would now be able to work with very skilled staff who had a good grounding in such things as the Ten Essential Shared Capabilities.[2] We believed our years of accumulated detailed knowledge and experience of what had helped and hindered our son's path to recovery would at last be recognised and put to good use. We assumed that Joe would be treated as an individual with complex needs who needed a great deal of warmth, understanding and humanity and that we, by this time a family in great distress but with invaluable experience, deserved to be given respect and empathy and regarded as a valued member of this new team. We were wrong – nothing could have been further from the truth.

It was now that it dawned on me that what had been going wrong for us as a family wasn't just a case of the private sector being led by the profit motive. We were dealing with an entire psychiatric system that was dysfunctional and needed fixing in a much bigger way than just 'tweaking' by improving communications with families. It made me realise how important my campaigning, training and consultancy work could be. I felt I was beginning to be in a position where I could now have some strategic influence.

So what does the future hold for Joe? We are now continuing with the family work which, although it still raises

---

2. A Department of Health framework for the mental health workforce with training materials on such things as 'Working in Partnership' and 'Promoting Recovery'. See also Appendix 2, p. 126.

big issues for us all, and has the potential to lead him into more distress and psychosis, we and the 'home team' believe is the only viable way forward. Until we have all enabled Joe to begin to process and make sense of what happened to cause his breakdown he will not be able to have a breakthrough. Through a remarkable individual I have met along the way, Joe now has a befriender of a similar age who has been through some dark times. He visits him regularly and provides a sense of companionship and normality to his life.

With the changes to the Mental Health Act that came into force in 2007, we have the possibility of a more holistic system, where respect, participation, least restrictive, alternative and appropriate treatment are enshrined in the law. There is also the potential in the future for a Responsible Clinician to be someone other than a psychiatrist. Because of these changes, the care coordinator is looking at the possibility of using an individualised budget to create a care package that genuinely meets Joe's needs and where he can have some choice in who he is with and what he does. This means ensuring that any future placements have thoughtful, psychologically aware staff who understand what we are all doing and are part of a team working collaboratively and valuing the contribution of everyone who knows and cares about our remarkable son. I know that he has great strengths and reserves and that he is still a thoughtful, sensitive human being with a great deal of potential who could use his experiences to make a real difference to the world one day. He deserves to be surrounded by other human beings who can see this and give him hope for a future that he can control. I firmly believe that now there is the opportunity to create the right network that will enable us all to turn this dream into a reality.

Helpful learning and information[3]

So how have I had the strength to continue on the long journey of recovery? The following factors have played a big part:

1. Having time initially to 'be with' Joe to begin to understand what he was going through and what helped.

2. Meeting other families going through similar experiences and knowing we were not alone.

3. Having an amazing Family Support Worker who gave me hope we would come through this nightmare and empowered me to become proactive to work to change the system.

4. Having a very talented worker in Joe's CMHT with lived experience that provided us with a role model of what is possible. He is the only one Joe really trusts. His thoughtful insights have helped us all through the dark times.

5. Being introduced to networks of individuals and groups who have a genuine understanding of mental distress and how alternatives to the medical model can make dramatic differences to people's lives.

6. Working to challenge and begin to change the system has given me a sense of purpose.

7. Being in positions of influence and being able use our family's experiences has at times been very therapeutic and liberating.

8. Work has also given us an extra income to have the opportunity to take breaks and do some more relaxing activities to give us the energy and stamina to continue on this long hard road.

3. This section also appears in Appendix 1 (p. 114) along with all other contributors' helpful learnings and essential information.

9. Knowing some positive and supportive people who understand the trauma and distress we are going through and have faith that we will all survive and thrive has given me continued strength and hope to continue.

HOPE
'Hope' is the thing with feathers –
That perches in the soul
And sings the tune without the words
And never stops – at all –

Emily Dickinson

Chapter 2
Loving Christian

Georgina Wakefield

PROUD

My youngest son, Christian John,
Suffers from schizophrenia
He suffers each day in silence
With a kind and gentle demeanour
But look deeply beyond his label
To the baby I held in my arms
To the cheeky mischievous 4 year old
Who captured the world with his charms
To the bright intelligent 10 year old
Who excelled at school in his study
To the 12-year-old football fanatic
Who'd come home exhausted and muddy
To the handsome carefree teenager
Who'd greet me each day with a kiss
To the son I'd lay down my life for
But the man I was destined to miss
He waded through the torment
Hallucinations and angry voices
Robbed of the sweet years of youth
And denied so many choices
He coped with public ignorance
And the pain inflicted by stigma
Accepting that mental illness
Is viewed as a kind of enigma

Because my son was sent on a journey
There were demons he had to face
Along with painful memories
He struggles each day to erase
Now he's quiet and unassuming
But to me he stands out in the crowd
He's the son he was always destined to be
And one word describes my feelings and that's
'Proud'

How can you put 18 years into one book chapter? Even the most powerful, well-chosen words seem to be inadequate, so I can only do my best. This chapter is in two halves, the first half concentrating on the bleak, early years, and how hard they were. The second is about recovery or as I see it, 'discovery', because that's what it is all about – discovering what works well and what doesn't. All carers go on this journey of discovery because we discover things about ourselves and carers also have to recover from this tragic life event themselves. First and foremost, carers have to learn acceptance, and it has taken me many years.

Another carer explained to me how she coped. She said:

> I was forever thinking/grieving about what life should have held in store for my son but if all of your life you've wanted to go to Italy only to find that you're going to Holland, thinking constantly about Italy serves no purpose simply because you miss the sights of Holland (windmills, scenery, tulips etc.). It's accepting that you're not going to Italy that proves to be the hardest part of all. It's also accepting that we are totally powerless over what happens to us, or indeed to people we love. All we can do is provide support, compassion and love.

My youngest son Christian developed paranoid schizophrenia at the age of 16. He is now 34. Life has, in 2009, finally reached a far more manageable and peaceful stage; the early years are now behind us. When I think about those early years I still shudder – the nights without sleep, the endless reassuring, the overwhelming sadness and grief. There are no words to adequately explain what it feels like to watch someone you love so dearly losing their mind right before your very eyes. Only those who have walked this walk can share this.

The early years

Initially, the confusion in itself was overwhelming. I was plagued by thoughts and questions. Is he just being a difficult teenager? I'm sure he's smoking cannabis. Is his behaviour down to the drugs? Or is this something far more sinister, for example, the beginnings of a severe mental health problem? Following 15 months of sheer hell and three visits to his GP, I was told twice that I'd have to bring him to the surgery in person. How was I expected to do that when my son had totally lost sight of reality and would tell me, 'It's you who's mad, not me'?

On the third visit a friend came with me – I was in bits by then – and she asked the GP if he thought Christian was mentally breaking down? 'I've no doubt that he is,' was the reply. To which my friend then said, 'How do you expect him to make a rational decision to come to the surgery if he's mentally breaking down? Those two things don't go together.'

With that, he finally sent two social workers to our home. After 20 minutes with Chris they said that within a fortnight he would have been sectioned anyway – as if I didn't know that. One of them said, 'He's very thin Mrs Wakefield, surely you must have noticed.' He was, of course, very thin – he weighed about 8 stones 2 pounds and at 6 feet 2 inches, but I was in far too much of a state to tell the social workers how difficult it was getting things through to his GP.

Then came the visit to the consultant psychiatrist who told us our son had a thought pattern disorder and that they were putting him on intramuscular injections of Piportil, four times a week. That was it, nothing more was said. We weren't warned about the effects that the drugs would have; for example, he started to sleep for 16 hours a day and walked around like a zombie with lead boots on.

We felt as if we were out in the wilderness for the next seven years. Life went on but Christian had no life, no friends, no fun, no holidays, no relationships. His friends abandoned him, one of them actually said to me: 'It's really sad but don't ask me to visit him.'

We took him on holiday and it was a disaster, he became more and more unwell by the day. When we got home his GP prescribed some tablets in addition to the Piportil, but they caused a dystonic[1] reaction, a side effect of the medication change. His whole body and face twisted up and we had no idea at all that this was even a possible 'side effect'. I rang his GP at 11pm. I was crying and extremely scared. I asked the doctor to come out because I thought my son was having a fit. He refused point blank and said to give him two Procyclidine tablets to counter the side effect of the other medication. I did, and it made no difference. Half an hour later I phoned him back and this time I begged him to come. When he entered our home Chris was in a ball on the floor still twisted up. He said we should pull ourselves together and

---

1. Dystonia is a syndrome of spasms and sustained contractions of the muscles. These muscle movements are not under voluntary control and they result in repetitive abnormal movements of parts of the body or persistently abnormal postures. Picked up off net doctor: www.netdoctor.co.uk/diseases/facts/**dystonia**.htm

get him over to Accident and Emergency (A&E) where they would 'zap' him. I asked him what he meant by 'zap'. 'They'll give him an injection which will release it,' he replied.

We took him (half carrying him) to A&E in our car. On the way he was trying to get out of the car by opening the door, but his brother just about managed to keep him in his seat by brotherly brute force. This was a very dangerous situation and the GP should have prevented that risk by calling an ambulance. I will never forget that night, I call it the worst night of my life simply because it was so horrific to witness a young man of 21 going through so much pain and anguish.

The psychiatrist prescribed Chris two other neuroleptics (Olanzapine and Ritanserin) to see if they would have any positive effect, but neither helped his condition so he was put back onto Piportil again. His brother, Steven, left home to live with his girlfriend in the May of 1997 and we didn't have a clue how much Chris would miss him. Steven was, by now, the only young person in his life.

Christmas 1997 was another disaster. Christian became very ill and two days after Christmas he relapsed and was admitted to an acute ward. After five weeks he was moved to a rehab centre – little did we know that he would stay there for the next five years.

We would visit him in the week and then have him home at weekends. When we went to see him for the first time our hearts sank; many of the residents were much older than him. There he sat, dressed smartly as always, looking extremely handsome and totally out of place. He would phone me constantly begging me to take him home but we knew we couldn't manage. Sometimes he would threaten to run away which pulled at our heartstrings. One sunny Friday evening I looked round at him in the car and the tears were streaming down his face. He told me that his head was all over the place and he didn't know how to straighten his thoughts out. I felt so very sad and thought, if only I could get inside his head and untangle the jumbled wiring to release him from his pain.

The months rolled into years. When Chris had been in rehab for almost two years my husband Paul and I attended a Rethink seminar in Chelmsford. Professor Adrianne Reveley was conducting a presentation during the lunch break. Afterwards I told her about Chris, now 25. I explained that he became ill at 16 and had been in care (in a rehabilitation centre to help him return to life in the community) for two years. She asked me if he had ever been tried on Clozapine? When I replied no she went on to explain that Chris was probably treatment resistant (TRS, Treatment Resistant Schizophrenia) and that Clozapine was the best medication for people who were TRS. And so, in 1999, seven years into his illness, and two years into his stay in rehab, he was prescribed Clozapine on a trial basis. He'd been tried on two other neuroleptics during the seven years but neither made any difference to his condition.

He'd been on it for about three weeks when Paul and I thought he seemed better. We were almost scared to believe it. Twelve weeks later Chris was moved into 12-hour care – a further step towards independence. He was to spend another two and a half years there.

A psychiatrist once said to me that recovery in mental illness is like a flower bulb in your hand – years later it's grown in size. It's just terribly slow – it is happening but you just can't see it.

As far as Chris was concerned, I do think it's far worse to develop this condition at such a young age, if you've had relationships, learnt to drive, held down a job, lived independently, you have all of those things to fall back on as you travel down the long road to recovery.

So finally, in September 2002, Christian was well enough to move into his own flat, a five-minute car journey from where we live. Just before he moved a hundred residents staged a protest at a junior school across the road from the flat stating: 'We don't want the mentally afflicted living near us.'

A colleague of mine who worked for the mental health charity Mind at the local branch drop-in went to a meeting organised by residents who were complaining. She said that people at the meeting were; 'like baying wolves', not allowing her or anyone else to speak about mental health problems. Several letters appeared in the local paper, one of them was headed 'Caring about Children' and read, 'It's because we care about children that we object to the type of people going into this complex, we'd have no objections at all to the physically disabled but we do object to the mentally ill because of the danger to our everyday lives.'

Christian read the letters and couldn't understand why people would judge him without even knowing who he is.

After a couple of months of settling in to his new flat Chris decided to start going swimming again; we were really pleased. He was going for about an hour, three times every week. One day one of the lifeguards called him out of the pool wanting to know why he went swimming so much. Chris told him the truth, that he'd had a mental illness and was trying to build up his muscles. Warning bells rang for me, whereas Paul thought the lifeguard was just being friendly. I had this gut feeling that something horrible was going to happen. The next time Chris went swimming he rang me at work. At first I didn't even know it was him because he was shivering and crying at the same time. He kept repeating 'what do they mean about children?' I managed to calm him down and was horrified to hear that two uniformed policemen had called him out of the pool and asked him, 'Why are you in there while there's children in there?' I can still feel those same feelings of disbelief and disgust to this day.

That day, Paul picked me up from work and the first stop was the swimming pool. I asked the manager what had prompted him to call the police. To my amazement he said it hadn't been him but the head teacher from the local school. I went to see the head teacher who told me that she was there to protect children. When I asked her what from, she repeated, 'I'm here to protect children.' Again I asked her from what? She replied: 'Well he sort of stands at the side of the pool for 10 minutes.'

I explained that Chris has problems making a decision and that he would be trying to decide whether to get out or stay in. At this point I felt we'd taken enough. This situation had occurred because my son made the mistake of telling the lifeguard that he had a mental illness and because of public ignorance. Christian didn't go swimming again until nine months had passed. If I suggested he went he'd say that he couldn't because he felt ashamed. This incident affected him so much that he had to start taking Prozac for severe depression – which we found hardly surprising since it's not every day you're practically accused of being a paedophile.

My feelings of anger and disgust remain within me and I am sure they always will.

The young police sergeant who called Chris out of the pool came to see us and openly admitted that he knew nothing at all about schizophrenia. I was amazed that this was someone who was likely to get called out to a young person going through their first psychotic breakdown and yet he knew nothing at all about what he would be dealing with.

As I explained earlier those were the bleak years and now it's time to move on to the better times.

Recovery

About two years ago Chris was offered a psychodynamic talking therapy, based on the concept of the 'other mind'. He has been having one-and-a-half-hour weekly sessions combined with art therapy. It began with one-to-one sessions and then progressed to group therapy. This has made an enormous difference, giving Chris a level of understanding over his condition so that he has a good insight into, and knows the difference between what's reality and what's delusional content from the 'other mind'.

We were also offered family therapy, and I joined a carer's group which was facilitated by a group analyst. There we all learned about our own 'other minds'.

Using the psychodynamic therapy with the concept of the 'other mind' has been hugely helpful both to my family and to my son. In our ignorance we arranged for Christian to see a cognitive behaviour therapy (CBT) counsellor but after five sessions he refused to go back explaining in his own words that 'it does my head in'. We were lucky enough to make contact with a psychiatrist who explained that patients need to be assessed to find out which therapy will work best and so Christian was finally assessed. CBT works on the basis of attempting to change our thoughts and as Christian is quite thought-disordered, we saw that CBT made matters worse in his case.

For example, in the assessment interview the psychiatrist was talking to Christian about his day-to-day concerns. She'd been talking to him about the 'other mind' and he was beginning to distinguish what was his healthy self and what was coming from the other mind. He was able to concentrate and express some of his current difficulties. When I entered the room with no warning he turned to me and said in a rather loud and complaining voice, 'You can't expect me to say more than this. Why do you always want me to be different? It's not fair.'

I felt uneasy and embarrassed. I tried to brush it off and said, 'It's OK Chris. I don't expect anything of you and I haven't even said anything.' The psychiatrist said, 'I think the other mind is telling you that your mother is criticising you even though she hasn't said a word.'

For a moment Christian was about to argue then suddenly his face changed and he smiled and with some relief said, 'You're right. I don't think she's criticising me at all.'

Together with the psychiatrist we decided to take a multi-pronged approach to a multifaceted condition. The first treatment in this approach was to be neuroleptic medication at the lowest possible dose – the psychiatrist explained that it had an important part to play. This was combined with attention to his diet. All too often sufferers resort to takeaways and processed foods, all of which add to poor general health.

The whole process of recovery is more one of 'discovery' – discovering what works well and what doesn't and finding a way to manage the painful symptoms. This emphasises the need-adapted treatment principle – that is, treatment adapted to each individual's needs. The third component of our recovery plan was family work with a family therapist who understands working in two minds. This understanding was a great relief to family and friends who live, or spend time with, the sufferer.

Another element of the treatment plan was psycho-education, which was incorporated into the assessment interview that we had initially with the psychiatrist. In the interview we were able to understand the principles behind Christian's treatment. This helped both at the time and later on when we had family therapy with a therapist who understood the treatment principles. This has been hugely helpful.

And finally, the psychodynamic therapy, incorporating the ideas of 'other mind', was the piece that completed the jigsaw for Christian. Of course other types of talking therapy might suit other people better.

So my conclusion from our experience as a family is that talking therapies are an essential part of the treatment of chronic psychosis. But they are not the only treatment as the illness affects many facets of a person's life.

Our experience tells us that it is essential to have long-term talking therapy available for people who have been suffering with mental health problems for years. So much more should be offered by a civilised society for the management and treatment of chronic psychosis. So let's get civilised …

Discovery or recovery?

Chris has done more in the past year than he did in the 17 years leading up to it. I believe this is all down to the factors I've described above and also having an excellent personal assistant, who has supported and interacted with him in so many positive ways. Direct Payments (see p. 125) provide another of the keys to mental well-being and social inclusion. It is not enough to rehabilitate people and then abandon them to 'treatment in the community', because it will lead to a revolving-door syndrome, isolation, depression and then of course relapse and back on the wards again. I call it 'feeding the spirit'. Recovery isn't just about the medical model, it's about human beings enjoying life, feeling part of society and regaining self-worth which has been destroyed by a devastating and debilitating condition.

Learning and information[2]

1. Love, support and compassion from family, friends and mental health professionals.

2. The right medication, tailored to suit individual needs.

3. Attention to diet.

4. Talking therapy, family therapy and carer therapy.

5. Paid part-time employment and support from work colleagues.

6. Independent living.

7. A befriender.

8. Pets (in Chris's case a dog and a talking parrot).

9. Exercise (walking, swimming).

10. Physical relaxation, for example, we bought a hot tub and this has helped Chris to relax.

11. Direct payments enabling the employment of the right personal assistant.

---

2. This section also appears in Appendix 1 (p. 115) along with all other contributors' helpful learnings and essential information.

Chapter 3
Neglect and abuse

Morgan Winterburn

The private sector

In the summer of 2007, my wife was feeling suicidal. Her psychiatrist felt she needed to be in hospital, and I agreed; however, because she worked in NHS mental health services, a bed needed to be found away from the area in which she worked. One was found in a unit run by a private sector mental health service provider.

Our first impressions were quite favourable: the staff were friendly, and there was a pleasant atmosphere. It felt almost more like a hotel than a mental health unit. Because of the risk of my wife attempting suicide, it was felt that someone had to be with her at all times, which meant them hiring agency staff to do this.

There was also concern about her ongoing problems with eating. However, staff got her some special rye bread (she has an allergy to wheat), and with their gentle support and encouragement, she started to make herself toast, and eat it (she had virtually stopped eating at home). This, for her, was significant progress.

The ward manager had been on leave when my wife was admitted. When she came back, she immediately insisted my wife be given full meals from the standard menu (or a vegan variant since my wife is vegan) instead. For my wife, whose relationship with food is problematic at best, this was incredibly threatening. However, the consultant overruled the ward manager, as he understood the difficulties my wife was experiencing. A compromise was agreed, which meant that my wife was offered a full meal at mealtimes but could refuse it and make herself some toast instead. In practice, this meant that a meal was always wasted (because she invariably refused it) but at least the ward manager could feel that her authority had not been undermined, and my wife could have what she felt confident to eat.

This went on for a number of weeks, and gradually my wife's spirits improved. She was making friends with the other patients, she was beginning to trust the staff, and her food intake was getting better too.

Then out of the blue one Friday I got a phone call from the unit, and was told that my wife had to be transferred somewhere else because they were having difficulty finding sufficient agency staff to do one-to-one observations with her. Over that weekend she was detained under Section 3 of the Mental Health Act because, not unnaturally, she did not want to go somewhere else she didn't know, and had tried to leave the unit.

At the ward round the following Monday we discussed this with the consultant and a nurse, and all agreed that the best thing was for her to remain at the unit. The consultant had just started her on a new medication, which he hoped would start to take effect within a few days, lowering her level of distress so that it would no longer be necessary for her to be on 24-hour one-to-one observation. The nurse also said that, despite the difficulties, they had always managed to find agency staff and there was no reason to believe that this would really be that much of a problem in future.

The next day the ward manager (who had been on leave the previous day when the ward round had taken place) rang me to say that my wife was being transferred to another of the private sector provider's units as soon as could be arranged. All my attempts to contact the consultant to discuss this sudden change of plan failed. Clearly, he didn't want to speak to me. I can only assume that, having overridden the ward manager once, he wasn't going to challenge her a second time.

So that Wednesday, I accompanied my wife to the new unit. The first one had been in a very affluent part of the country, and mainly catered for people from that area. The new place was in a deprived inner-city area. It was a low-level secure unit for people with complex needs. As soon as I went through the door, my spirits sank. It seemed more like a prison, certainly not a place where my wife could find the help and support she needed. We were taken to my wife's room; it was bare and bleak, with a couple of shelves, a bed, and no chairs. We discovered that here, two people would observe my wife at all times, not just one. This is something my wife found quite threatening. My wife pleaded with me to take her away, but of course I couldn't. She whispered to me that she would not be able to eat or even drink anything here, as it wasn't a place where she felt remotely safe.

The next day when I visited I saw her wailing in anguish in the corridor. When she saw me, she clung to me desperately. Because she had self-harmed by cutting herself in the past, they insisted that when she was in bed, her arms must be outside the covers at all times. How they thought she could harm herself under the covers with two people watching her constantly remains a mystery. My wife has osteoarthritis, which makes it very painful to hold her arms in such an unnatural position. Her arthritis also makes her much more susceptible to cold than most people, adding further to her pain and distress at being forced to do this. My attempts to talk to the staff, pointing out that this was abusive, and almost certainly contravened the Disability Discrimination Act, were ignored. It is interesting that one of the examples of the abuse of detainees at Guantanamo Bay given in press reports is that they were forced to keep their arms outside their bedclothes at all times.

After my visit to my wife had ended, the ward manager took me to one side and asked my advice about how she could be encouraged to eat and drink. I explained that the problem was she didn't feel safe there. I also pointed out that she had a supply of bottled water that was brought with her from the other unit (she only feels safe drinking a particular brand of bottled water – she can't bring herself to drink tap water), as well as a couple of loaves of rye bread, which she could eat toasted. When I spoke to my wife on the phone that night, she told me that they had found the bread and water in her luggage, told her that she wasn't allowed plastic bottles in her room and taken the water away, and had thrown the rye loaves out.

At the suggestion of an independent advocate, who had also visited my wife on that day, and who had been appalled at the brutal, bullying attitude of staff there, I contacted a solicitor who specialised in the mental health field. He agreed to visit my wife the next day, Friday.

I found out later that during the Thursday night my wife had a severe pain in the side of her face, and asked to see a doctor. The two staff with her refused to call a doctor. In a desperate attempt to summon aid, she started screaming. Her screaming was ignored; no one came.

On Friday morning when I visited my wife again, I found her lying on her bed in a state of extreme distress. By now she was too weak to walk, because she had been unable to eat or drink anything for some 48 hours. Earlier that morning, when it was time to take her medication, she had told the two staff with her that she couldn't walk down the corridor to the window where tablets were dispensed. They said to her that if she couldn't walk, she'd have to crawl. So she tried to crawl out of her room. When she reached the doorway to her room, a patient who was passing in the corridor poured a cup of coffee all over her (fortunately it was only lukewarm, or she would have been badly scalded).

When this happened, she collapsed so that her body was partly on a soft pouffe that had been specially brought in for staff to sit on when they were doing two-to-one observation; one of the staff deliberately moved the pouffe away from my wife so she would have nothing soft to lie on, just the hard floor. Both staff refused to help her up, claiming the organisation's moving and handling policy wouldn't allow it, and left her lying on the floor, in intense distress, soaked in coffee, for a couple of hours until I arrived at the unit. At which point the organisation's moving and handling policy mysteriously changed, because they then helped her on to the bed so that I wouldn't find her on the floor.

At the same time I arrived, the solicitor rang to inform the ward that he would be arriving in a few minutes. When the staff who were with my wife were told this, I witnessed them trying to persuade her to change her coffee-soaked nightdress for a clean one. Clearly, it wouldn't do for a solicitor to see a patient in such a state! She refused. When the solicitor came, he took one look at her and immediately demanded an ambulance be called to take my wife to Accident and Emergency. I am convinced that this is the only thing that saved my wife's life.

While we waited for the ambulance, the ward manager came into the room and told me visiting time was up. I refused to leave. Then she said the doctor was waiting in the nurses' office to speak to me; again I refused to leave my wife's side. I am convinced this was a ploy, and that if I'd left the room where my wife lay I'd have been ejected from the premises; one thing that convinces me of this is that the doctor later came in to give my wife a perfunctory examination, and showed no sign whatever of wanting to speak to me in private.

Eventually the ambulance arrived and took us, and two staff from the private hospital to observe my wife, to the local general hospital. Then began five days of desperate struggle to extricate my wife from the clutches of the private sector organisation before doctors in the general hospital finished their tests and sent her straight back there. This was difficult because my wife was still detained under the Mental Health Act, which meant that only the doctor responsible for her detention could agree to transfer her to back to NHS mental health services. This person also happened to be the director of the private facility, so he of course had a financial interest in keeping her in his power! During all that time I stayed at my wife's bedside (with brief meal breaks/comfort breaks), to protect her from the attentions of the two staff from the private facility who were there (in shifts) 24 hours a day.

How we got her out was as follows: a junior doctor and the ward manager from the private facility agreed to reassess her. The manager of the NHS general ward (who was incredibly supportive of us, once she understood the situation) told them that, given my wife's physical state, she could not sanction my wife going anywhere that didn't have ready access to the facilities of a general hospital. As the local NHS mental health facility was on the same site as another general hospital, and the private facility was nowhere near a general hospital, the director had no alternative but to agree to my wife's transfer back to the NHS.

There was one final twist of the knife, when the private organisation agreed to transport my wife to the NHS site. When their minibus arrived, it was driven by the manager of the ward where my wife had been abused. She claimed that their insurance would not cover them transporting a third party (me). There was no way we were going to allow her and the two staff 'observing' my wife to take her without me: my wife was terrified. I had to dash back to the general ward (leaving my wife with a helpful student nurse from that ward who promised she would not let them take my wife away without me) and get the ward manager to accompany me back to the car park, where there was a stand-off between the two ward managers; eventually the manager of the private ward backed down and agreed to make an 'exception' and take me with them.

Interestingly, when we got to the NHS facility, they didn't put her on continuous observation at all, just looked into her room every few minutes to check she was safe. Which she was. Finally.

The NHS inpatient unit

In 2008, my wife's mental health worsened again, and she agreed to go to hospital – to the same NHS mental health facility where she had ended up after the nightmarish experience of the private sector. Given my wife's problems with food (as I've mentioned, she is vegan, allergic to wheat, and drinks only bottled water), the ward manager had, on the previous admission, agreed that I would bring in food and water, and be reimbursed on presenting the receipts – a system that had worked reasonably well.

This time, there was a new acting ward manager. She told me that the previous arrangement was now cancelled, because their catering services should be able to provide all her dietary requirements. I agreed (I didn't have much option), and accepted her word that they would provide the items of food and drink my wife specified on a list that we gave the acting ward manager.

The following evening, a Friday, I rang my wife, and she told me that the catering manager had refused to supply her with anything on the list, including water. She hadn't had anything to eat or drink for 24 hours. I dashed out to the local supermarket to get her some supplies, then just managed to catch the bus to the hospital to get them to her so she wouldn't perish from dehydration (at that time of the evening buses are only one an hour, and I don't drive).

The next Monday I rang up and asked to speak to the Chief Executive of the Trust that provides mental health services in our area. He rang me back within the hour, listened to what I had to say about what had happened, and said he'd sort it out. He did. Later that day I was contacted by a senior catering manager who apologised and put a simple system in place whereby I could get reimbursed for the food and water I bought for my wife. That simple apology made all the difference. However, no such apology was ever given by the acting ward manager who had caused the problem in the first place.

My wife spent several months on that ward. In the main, most staff were supportive, most of the time. However, three things are worth noting. Firstly, on one occasion when my wife had her hair washed by a member of staff, they neglected to dry it or comb it out properly. Because of my wife's arthritis, she was unable to do this for herself. As a result, her long beautiful hair became tangled and matted, and no one was subsequently able to repair the damage. Months later, after she had discharged herself (about which, more later) she ended up having to cut most of it off as a result, which is something she found extremely traumatic as she'd always been very proud of her long hair. So a moment's thoughtlessness by a (no doubt busy) member of staff led to my wife experiencing huge and ongoing distress.

Secondly, while my wife was lying in bed in her room one day, her wedding and engagement rings were stolen by another patient. This was because she had been ordered by staff to leave her door ajar at all times whenever she was in her room 'for safety's sake'. Staff did nothing to try to get them back, and the rings were never recovered. Naturally she was extremely upset about this.

Thirdly, during this admission, staff did not find the time to accompany my wife to the kitchen (patients are not allowed into the kitchen unsupervised) so that she could make herself something simple to eat, such as porridge. As a result, even though I kept bringing in supplies, towards the end of her stay she virtually stopped eating. This caused immense problems when she had left hospital and tried to get back to a normal routine of eating.

One day, a junior doctor who had recently started on the ward examined my wife. She was not satisfied with the junior doctor's behaviour and attitude towards her, and said so. The junior doctor, instead of accepting this intended constructive criticism at face value, wrote an account of what happened in my wife's notes that differed from my wife's account. There was a multidisciplinary meeting (at which neither of us were present) at which it was decided that from then on, no member of staff would be able to see my wife without another staff member present. Our protests about this were ignored.

That weekend when I was visiting my wife I witnessed how this system operated. One member of staff came in to the room to give her her medication, while another hovered obtrusively in the doorway. It freaked me out, so I can only imagine how it was for my wife on other occasions when, for example, in distress in the middle of the night she tried to summon help and got two people coming to her room not one. It must have completely destroyed any chance she had of getting support or reassurance. Also, it must have vividly brought back to her the horrific experience of the private hospital, when two people were with her at all times.

Why did they do this? The only answer I can think of is that, faced with two different versions of what happened, the team decided that the trainee doctor's wish not to be challenged about her practice took precedence over the patient's well-being. So, I imagine staff saying to themselves, it is the trainee doctor's version that must be believed, and if the patient's account is different, then the patient must be lying or deluded, even though we've never known her to lie about anything before this, and for 'her own protection' (which is what they said to us – they never admitted it had anything to do with the 'protection' of staff from allegations of malpractice) we'll only see her in twos from now on.

The irony is, my wife had never had any intention of making a complaint, until the junior doctor and the rest of the staff made it such a big issue. After a few days of it, my wife found this treatment so unhelpful and distressing that she discharged herself from hospital and came home.

The Community Mental Health Team

My wife's community psychiatric nurse left her job in December 2008. This CPN tried to get a replacement Care Coordinator for her before she left, and identified someone, but unfortunately that person was not suitable. My wife sensed she had a patronising, judgemental attitude – which I saw for myself on the one occasion I met her. So my wife tactfully explained that she didn't feel she could work with her, and we left it at that.

One other thing her CPN did before she left was to arrange for a private care agency to come in twice a day while I was out at work. By this time, my wife's ongoing physical problems meant that she had difficulty getting about the house, and could not use stairs unaided. The agency helped her with personal care, such as washing, as well as various simple tasks about the house that my wife was unable to do. This was intended to be a temporary arrangement until my wife was feeling stronger, but unfortunately the hoped-for improvement in my wife's physical health has not yet happened.

Then one day, two people from the CMHT, one of whom was the team manager, came to see her. Despite my wife asking, prior to this visit, what the purpose of the visit was, they refused to tell her. It was only when they were in our home that they informed her why they were there. They were there to tell her the care agency wouldn't be coming any more, with immediate effect. There was no discussion, no assessment of my wife's current needs, no acknowledgement of any risk to my wife that might result from this, no consideration of what effect it might have to take away the only service currently being given to someone who had made a number of suicide attempts in the past and who was known to be extremely depressed at the time.

What followed was a nightmare for us both. With the care agency withdrawn, I was unable to do my job properly. Each day I would go to the office, answer emails for a couple of hours, and print off papers to read at home, before dashing back to try to look after my wife. Sometimes I would get to a meeting, always aware that I would have to dash home again immediately after. Fortunately I had very understanding managers.

During this time I was desperately trying to contact every agency I could think of to get support for my wife. I also had several telephone conversations with the person who had accompanied the team manager on that visit. It turned out she was the lead for social care in the CMHT. She revealed that the person my wife had informed the CMHT she couldn't work with had actually been assigned as her Care Coordinator ever since my wife's CPN had left. This person had never done anything to address my wife's needs, and no one had bothered to let my wife know she was her Care

Coordinator – we'd both assumed that her psychiatrist was her 'default' Care Coordinator in the absence of anyone else. My wife and I were stunned at the sheer arrogance of this.

When asked for an explanation why they had stopped the care agency, the social care lead claimed there had been 'difficulty in identifying regular personal care needs' for the care agency staff.

Earlier I explained how my wife had discharged herself from the NHS ward because, as I explained earlier, they had decided no member of staff should see my wife on their own. At the time, we thought this decision was specific to the ward. But evidently this was not the case and the message had gone out far and wide to all health services that *no health professional must ever see my wife on their own under any circumstances!* No one ever had the decency to actually inform my wife about this decision. So, when my wife had a couple of brief admissions to the General Hospital, two nurses appeared at the bedside whenever my wife needed anything and a much-needed district nurse visit was delayed by weeks, because the district nurses had been told they had to turn up at our home in twos and they didn't have enough staff to do this when we needed them most. And the care agency was instructed to send two people for every visit.

Now, imagine two agency staff coming in to our home twice a day. One person could cater to my wife's personal needs such as washing. The other person was there simply because the CMHT had decreed it, not because we wanted it – and sometimes there was not much for this second person to do. This, according to the social care lead, was why the care agency had been withdrawn!

At this point I should reveal that, like my wife, I work for the NHS, in mental health services. I work for the same organisation, in fact, that currently provides mental health services to my wife. During this nightmare time I offloaded to a deputy manager in my team about what we were going through, and she asked whether I would mind if she spoke to the social care lead about the situation herself (the deputy manager is a social worker by background).

A few days later, the social care lead told me that the care agency would be reinstated, to be reviewed after a month. But this time, only one person would be coming, twice a day. Whether this means they are now prepared for financial reasons to make an exception to the otherwise universal rule that two people must see my wife at all times, or whether that rule has finally been rescinded, I have no idea. As I write this, the social care lead is due to visit us next week, to discuss my wife's needs. My wife fears they are going to take the care agency away again.

It seems clear to me that all my attempts as a carer to get the care agency reinstated or to get other help for my wife counted for absolutely nothing. The only thing that worked was my deputy manager having a quiet chat with her colleague, because she saw that I couldn't do my job properly (and how stressed I was about the situation).

Though we have met my wife's psychiatrist and other CMHT staff several times since she discharged herself from the inpatient ward last November (I'm writing this in April 2009) there has been no care plan or any formal care planning meeting during all that time. The latest care plan my wife has received was dated October 2008, while she was an inpatient, and contained a number of major inaccuracies. The last time we saw her psychiatrist, we thought it was going to be a proper care planning meeting, but on the day he informed us it was instead a 'feedback session' (whatever that means).

So for over five months my wife, someone who is extremely distressed and extremely vulnerable, has been left without a proper care plan, with no one doing anything to address her serious and complex needs. Apart from the care agency (who have given us a good service but who are not mental health professionals) and some limited input from district nurses, we've been left to cope on our own. How can this happen in 2009?

Finally, it is salutary to note that both my wife and I are employed to promote service user involvement in mental health services. If we get such appalling treatment from mental health services, despite all our efforts and 'inside knowledge' of how mental health services operate, what hope can there be for anyone else?

Chapter 4
Memories, medication and meaning in manufacturing madness

Marion Hughes

I am a single-parent mother who became a carer when my daughter Jane developed mental health problems while she was a second-year undergraduate at a university about 150 miles away. This was nine years ago at the time of writing.

I returned home late one night and found Jane's tearful request to come to collect her on the answerphone. I returned her call and recognised immediately how odd she sounded. However, I was still totally unprepared for the shock of seeing Jane the next day as she lay inert in bed, unaware of why I was there, almost unrecognisable as the girl I had known up until then. Subsequently, I learned from her housemates that for some weeks, Jane had been behaving and speaking strangely, neglecting her course work, avoiding company, not eating, not sleeping, weeping in isolation in her room, neglecting her own personal hygiene, inevitably jeopardising her own safety, particularly in late night wanderings. Her normally organised room was untidy, the floor randomly littered with clothing, books and papers. I now know these are all clear symptoms of someone with mental health problems and they should have been recognised by her tutors and student health services.

Jane had become so completely different from the confident, sociable, lively daughter I had known – I thought she was clearly ill, and I was upset that no one had contacted me, her main support throughout her life to date. Her personal tutor, the Student Health Service and the GP to whom she had been referred, had all respected her right to confidentiality. Her university GP did not know her but had advised her to attend the drug rehabilitation unit, an option she refused since she wasn't taking street drugs. This is the first point at which the system let Jane down, when trained professionals failed to consider the range of possible diagnoses. The tension between family needs and professional needs was further highlighted when it seemed, that to the helping professionals, whatever happened to her in her state of vulnerability, whatever abuse, even up to and including her possible death, was unimportant compared to her assumed wish of a right to confidentiality. Her views were not sought. It was a situation I was to meet countless times, in many ways and variations, in the nine years since.

Professionals think that no situation is too trivial or too serious to breach the sacred barrier of corporate 'confidentiality'. It is noteworthy that, conversely, carers are afforded *no* confidentiality by psychiatric staff. The system seems carefully orchestrated for maximum conflict, upset and confusion within a family already greatly stressed.

Of course I do not need, nor do I want, to know every detail about my adult daughter's life – that would be entirely inappropriate – but I need to know enough to be able to help and support her in the best way in a crisis. Whatever danger Jane is in, no one will warn me, no one will discuss ways of helping us manage together whatever disaster has happened, or what might develop subsequently. It makes no sense. When estranging patients from family and social contacts, services see 'independence' as the ultimate goal. Why? Most of us recognise we are social animals and *interdependence* is the social normality not reclusiveness; indeed it is an essential prerequisite for survival. It is widely recognised that successful recovery of mental health requires a core support group of five to six people who are *not* mental health paid workers.

Jane was sectioned and admitted to the psychiatric hospital within days of her coming home. In the early weeks, I went through a state of denial, disbelieving what was happening, an experience I now know to be familiar to all new families in this situation. This is a nightmare. I must wake up soon. What has happened to the life I had? It seemed that Jane had disappeared behind a thick veil or fog; occasionally there were glimpses of the girl I knew but then they vanished like a will-o'-the-wisp. If I tried to talk to ward staff, I met their blank indifference; I was in shock and did not know how to interpret this weird, cold reaction. This was new, an aloof response to this distress wasn't human; we had become 'non-people'. Was the hospital really offering help, support and recovery, or not?

Jane was given a huge wodge of written information (the 'Welcome Pack') on admission to the ward – some of it of most relevance to the family. However, the family is unlikely to see it since it is buried amongst policies, protocols, procedures and practices – so much bumph, so finely printed, in difficult legalese and probably all unread by the patient, particularly when he or she is in a confused, upset state, coupled with the trauma of recent admission. It may be an example of complying with the law, but it does so in a tick-box way that neither relates to the patient's nor the carer's situation.

It felt as if no one acknowledged the love and concern I had for my daughter; how this is a continuing lifetime commitment and how crucially important it is for both of us. If some disaster happens, it will have a lifetime impact on both of us, while for the professionals, it may scarcely merit a comment, an incident perhaps logged, but soon forgotten. The inhumanity of impersonal disinterest, the lack of awareness, sometimes the outright contempt for the carer or family shown by some mainstream mental health staff, still astonishes and frustrates me. The emotional impact of the loss of a loved friend or relative to mental illness is ignored, and the persistent, often agonising sadness, continuing through the years, frequently for decades, is not recognised at all. Indeed, there may be suspicion (even outright accusation) that the carer or family have caused the problem. Family abuse can and does cause serious mental health problems, but this does not apply to most families. Shockingly cruel suggestions and statements may come from professionals, family, friends, and sometimes from the service user.

Many carers are left alone to find their own way, however they can, through this morass of grief. Companionship and comfort can be found at times with other carers on the same journey, but rarely does help come from professionals. More often than not the carer is abandoned, entirely alone. Statutory services, especially, fail to recognise the catastrophic effects of the long-term stress on the health of the carer. The unpredictable and rapidly changing nature of mental health problems are relentless, unremitting and continue for years, perhaps decades. There is no switch-off time, no time waking or sleeping when I am unaware of the imminence of crisis if not immersed in it. I am anxious leaving for a day's break, even sometimes just for a few hours. Recently, I spent a weekend away with other carers, and I noticed how someone in the group was always on her mobile phone checking the situation back home. No professional ever seems to ask, 'How would I feel if it were me?' 'What would I want if this were my beloved son/daughter/spouse?' They seem to lack empathy.

It seems connected to the stigma surrounding mental health issues. I feel very much for the discomfort and embarrassment of old friends with children of a similar age to Jane who enthuse about their children's successes, then enquire about Jane. They don't know what to do, or what to say, they cannot imagine how it must be for me, and then they disappear – not unkindly, but awkwardly, not knowing how to continue. Quite often, we never meet again. It does not seem to be in anyone's job description to understand and assist distraught families and alleviate the toll on their own health. Eventually, I am told, some 50–70% of carers become mental health service users themselves; a truly horrifying indictment of the lack of support offered to them at an earlier stage.

I not only see my beloved girl suffering as my daughter, but also as another human being, and I am desperate to help her and others suspended in similar limbo. I felt inadequate, since this was a situation of which I had no prior experience – I had no information and no idea where to find any. Not only could I not help my daughter, I could not even help myself. All I could do immediately was to be there, even though I was rejected, treated dismissively, or ignored by staff, and attacked physically or verbally – sometimes both – by my confused daughter.

Once a mental illness has been recognised and 'diagnosed', the conventional mainstream approach currently is to mask it with neuroleptic medication, i.e., sedate the patient, suppressing and containing the symptoms, without tackling the causes. Jane's psychiatrists appear to have no interest in her history, and ignore its relevance to the ongoing situation in terms of the significance of anniversary dates etc., and her particular vulnerability at such times – in fact, Jane's traumatic background story is all dismissed as part of the 'psychosis', although I have provided a written history. I know these events are *not* the product of a troubled imagination, they are real and there was tangible proof of some of them even while Jane was on the ward. They include rape, one as a child and one which resulted in pregnancy and miscarriage (the miscarriage occurred while she was on the ward). This would be enough to cause severe disturbance in some people, but then Jane's life was further blighted when she went to help a young woman being harassed by a street gang and was then abducted and held captive by the gang, in fear of her life.

The relation of traumatic events to mental health problems is increasingly recognised by more enlightened psychiatrists, but not yet by the mainstream majority. As Dorothy Rowe states, 'The presenting problem is never the real problem. In mental distress, the real problem always arises from some kind of threat or insult to the sense of being a person' (www.psychminded.co.uk, comment article dated 9 October 2008).

The approach here was, and remains, to put people on drugs and leave them on drugs, unless they qualify for Early Intervention (EI). EI has now been introduced in the hospital to which my daughter was admitted, but too late for her and so many like her, because here, EI is not offered to anyone known to services for more than two years.

My worst nightmare is that I should provoke relapse or worse by challenging my daughter's comments, no matter how unfair or untrue they may be. Part of me knows that by not challenging I am supporting an unreal view, and that's also a dangerous strategy when we're trying to achieve recovery. Neither do I know whether it is conscious manipulation on her part or is now part of the tangle of real history, nightmares and drugged confusions. I am angry about the unfairness, and at my own silence, if my beloved daughter really now believes I am the architect of her wasted life. What do I do – confront and challenge it or just accept it?

Of course, I can never be certain whether some early critical event in family life might have made a difference. If I'd recognised and addressed it, perhaps this mental illness might have been avoided. My torments are as endless as they are pointless; I did my best at all times in the circumstances in which I found myself.

I am angry about the social injustice that sees my daughter's life laid waste while those who traumatised her, devastating her life and mine, go free, and 'the system' anaesthetises her rather than listens and restores her life to her with appropriately tailored psychological support.

I am angry, too, that life on the wards is so boring and unproductive. Smoking is the main activity, together with all-day TV with all its violence, crises, catastrophe films and distressing news stories. The telescreen cannot be turned off between 8 am and midnight and much TV appears to be currently obsessed with psychopathic behaviour. How are these activities supposed to help people who are confused, frightened, trying to cope with internal thought disorders and who may be paranoid? To me, it is obvious that such a brutalising media diet re-traumatises people who have in many cases already experienced similar abuses. As this is the most widely based ward activity, I would like to see the research supporting its therapeutic value, since all practices should be evidence-based these days. Visitors have to compete with the telescreen and meetings have to be conducted in shared public space, as there is no private family visiting space.

I am distressed because no one helps me to cope and angry because my beloved daughter is dumped, discarded and subjected to the stigma and cruelty of an uncaring, ignorant and impersonal society. As a carer, I get the same treatment too. We have become social lepers. We are supposed to live in an anti-discriminatory culture, and anti-stigma campaigns are common, yet discrimination is widespread, with NHS staff too, although these are people who are supposedly trained to be sensitive to, and prevent, discrimination.

I am angry because seemingly impenetrable barriers imprison the daughter I brought up, and worsen as she's ineffectively drugged as 'treatment'. I am frustrated with myself for not being able to offer the support to achieve Jane's recovery when I want this so desperately.

Other frustrations include the way patients taking 'leave' from the ward are dealt with. Patients considered for leave are invariably the last to be seen by the consultant in the ward round. Carers are asked to be there for 9 am although the patient may not be interviewed until 12 noon or later, and the consultant may exclude the carer from the interview even when the patient has particularly asked for him/her to be present. If medication is not available until 5 pm, as commonly happens, the whole day's 'leave' has been spent hanging about the hospital. Sometimes, if medication has not arrived by 5 pm, it's even suggested that the patient stays until the next morning. The hospital in which Jane has spent so much time was formerly an isolation hospital. It is remote, accessible easily only by car (with substantial parking charges for every visit). Public transport is infrequent, circuitous and takes a long time. A sequence of several buses may be required, with each stage taking almost an hour. A taxi costs about £10 for a single trip. Every feature of this suggests a complete disregard for both patient and carer, or for any other responsibilities, problems or commitments they may have or financial constraints – the hospital routine is the only consideration.

I am left thinking that some people who choose to work with vulnerable people are attracted to the position of power it gives them. Last year, I explored alternatives for my daughter and found an opportunity that really enthused her. However, she lost interest when a member of ward staff said, 'Forget about moving on. It will be years, if ever, before you recover.' That offhand demolition of hope had me spluttering with rage. How dare anyone destroy hope like that? That may seem quite a small incident, but when someone's self-esteem and confidence are so undermined, it has a devastating effect and its continuing impact has been enormous. It destroyed the vitality that had returned to Jane's face and body language, and it's still missing.

Clearly not all staff exhibit this casual cruelty. I have met many kindly staff, many frustrated people who are distressed that they are not able to do the job they intended and wanted to do. When I see the locked ward doors, and know how my comments are ignored and I am marginalised, I want to know who oversees and reports what's really happening, since self-assessment and reporting is the accepted practice. The only reliable route for complaints from mental health patients and their carers is contacting the chief executive. The system is very protective of itself, some middle managers are like black holes, blocking complaints, enquiries and investigation as they never reply, or fail to follow up with promised actions; some admit they haven't spent a day on the wards in decades.

The contrast with the models of shared management, education and discussion for cancer and diabetes patients and their families, and my recent experience of orthopaedic surgery and after-care in the NHS, couldn't be more marked. I cannot understand why it is so different for mental health services.

People with mental health problems are often sent 'home' from the ward (i.e., to the parents' or family home, *not* his or her own home) without prior notice or discussion and on the assumption that this will be entirely acceptable. The inconvenience is often extreme, but cannot be conveyed to the service user in their vulnerable state. Plans to go out to dinner, theatre, go away, visit friends, or other commitments all have to be cancelled discretely at the last minute.

Many of the more enlightened staff in this Trust have

moved to work in Early Intervention (EI). I'm glad that patients are being helped more sympathetically and that the EIP (Early Intervention in Psychosis) service is better resourced. However, as I mentioned previously, it leaves my daughter (amongst others), rejected for EI because she has been too long in the system. In addition, mainstream services are now even more depleted, with fewer trained or motivated staff, and it seems (in my observation) fewer resources for, and staff with genuine belief in, recovery – despite official government recovery policies and promotion.

Recently, beds have been removed and wards closed as required by government directive, and this at a time when bed occupancy was around 120% locally – hardly spare capacity. As resources for care in the community have not been increased, and were already overstretched last year, the only remedy is to anaesthetise patients with drugs, leaving them unattended, isolated, locked away behind their own front doors. This is not my idea of therapy.

I have concern because, having addicted the patient to prescribed drugs, most staff have little or no training and experience of how to reduce or withdraw medication successfully. There are few rehabilitation facilities (none locally), and nowhere to help prescribed drug-addicted patients come off drugs safely. Neuroleptic drugs are powerful and can have very negative side effects, including some of the symptoms popularly associated with 'psychosis' and permanent brain damage.[1]

Care in the community in practice means more responsibilities are dumped on the carer without any discussion. On one occasion, I returned from about 400 miles away to find Jane drugged and barely surfacing when

1. For more information on neuroleptic and other psychoactive drugs, see *A Straight Talking Introduction to Psychiatric Drugs* by Joanna Moncrieff in this series.

'the team' (two people) arrived with the next drug dose. They came three times a day, so she was visited by six people every day. None had looked in the kitchen and seen there was no food, or recognised that Jane, anaesthetised by the drugs, was incapable of making a meal. Jane herself had no idea when she'd last eaten.

Community-based support workers are often casual in their approach to appointments, cancelling meetings at the last minute or just not turning up; they seem to assume that the service user has nothing else to do anyway, so it won't matter. Sometimes they ignore emergency calls for help repeatedly. These are unacceptable practices.

The process of grieving can have some positive attributes. The patient and carers feel the loss of a life of promise – all the possibilities that were available until the advent of mental health problems. The carer has a particular sense of his own lost life too. Yet it is often only the carer who hangs on to the tantalising little spark of hope that recovery is possible. People do recover, even after decades. Furthermore, no matter how remote we seem to be from our loved ones at times, we are tenacious, we remain there for them. They are in our consciousness from first waking, and they appear in our dreams and nightmares. I never fail to be astounded by the generosity, selflessness and humanity of the carers I know, and their empathy for others in that situation. I know I am privileged to know such stalwarts.

What was particularly helpful?

Empathic companionship
Having someone to share difficult times – sometimes just to listen to the grief, sometimes just to share the silence beyond words, and sometimes to share laughter too has been, at times, a lifesaver. I know there are no quick fixes, but a

confidante (or several ideally) who is there for me, a companion at the worst times, sometimes helping by planning a distraction, a short break away, a visit to the theatre, a film, a talk, music, a walk in the country by a river, stream or the sea, a weekend exploring a new place, these distractions and these people have been crucial supports for me. Carers inhabit a strange alternative universe known only by those who have been diverted onto the mental illness journey, those who have known the alienation of a loved person staring at you as if you were a malevolent stranger. Even if you recognise this as an effect of neuroleptic drugs blocking emotional responses, associated with the pre-frontal lobes of the cerebral cortex, it is most upsetting – and you don't know that initially. No one tells you. Nor do you know if those changes will be permanent. The fears and pain need to be shared.

Wellness and Recovery Action Plan (WRAP)

A helpful activity is the Wellness and Recovery Action Plan (WRAP),[2] and its variations. Sometimes, this starts as a group venture; and the group might include a mix of service users, carers and, quite often, support workers as well. However, an individual may choose to do a WRAP on their own, and all other variations have worked too; it's whatever works for each person. WRAP is a resource file of personal strategies, like problem-solving approaches which work for that individual, supportive contacts, activities, quotations, compliments, other people's views of you, special mementoes, etc., whatever helps, organised in specified sections for easy referral at difficult times. A WRAP is just as useful for carers, indeed, anyone going through a difficult time, not just service users.

2. Information can be found at http://www.mentalhealthrecovery.com/shop/index.php

WRAP derives from the work of Mary Ellen Copeland (see footnote), an American service user who wanted to help herself recover from mental illness. When her consultant was at a loss to suggest anything she could do for herself, she took the initiative, sent out an Internet message and compiled all the techniques people had found worked for them.

This initiative has now developed further in some Trusts, which publish a number of very delightful and useful 'Recovery Plan' booklets. These are worked on and managed by the patient and, if he chooses, perhaps might be shared, in part or whole, with supporting staff, friends and family. They are not a substitute for care plans, but supplement them and encourage people to think in a different way and take back control of their lives, as the booklets are entirely about recovery.

At best, WRAP-based materials need to create a living, working document, not something done as a one-off exercise then left on the shelf. The WRAP can relate to any possible problem and will change as the situation changes and the person progresses, so a strategy that works well at one time may be superseded later. The value of discussion – as a group initially – is that other people will share what has been useful for them, and therefore might be for you; and you will jog each other's memories, so it's a valuable starting point. Also, being in a group helps focus the mind at a particular time, it breaks the isolation as people recognise we all have many problems in common, and there will also be some laughter to share. I will refer to the special value of groups again, later.

Stemming from my WRAP, I found that I wanted to include messages, letters, birthday cards, pictures, drawings, photos, inspirational or helpful quotes and the file became too bulky, so I decided to develop my own 'personal file of delights' – I have loved putting it together, and this is a continuing project. Looking through it lifts a bad day, reminding me of wonderful friends, family and times.

A splinter group from WRAP meets locally each week to enable people to talk in a safe environment about their feelings. This is particularly valuable for people who may never have had confidantes or opportunities to reflect honestly and openly about their feelings. To do so knowing that no one will be sitting in judgement is a rare freedom. It is an opportunity for exploring feelings and finding links between the thoughts which preceded those feelings and the behaviours which resulted. Making the crucial links between thoughts, feelings and behaviour helped me regain some control of my life, no longer reacting on automatic pilot. The thoughts, feelings, behaviour sequence trips along very quickly, but not instantaneously. Once I recognised the chain reaction, it was possible to change a long-term behaviour pattern triggered by an entrenched thought which was no longer relevant. And that opens the way for new behaviours.

Organised groups, societies, communities for sharing information and experience are invaluable
I have found that the best groups for carers offer four types of help. There is some degree of overlap and all are important:

1. The simplest is of the entertainment, 'switch-off,' short-breaks variety.

2. Self-care opportunities – alternative therapies top this list, dealing with stress, anxiety, anger, self-esteem and confidence building.

3. Education about specific aspects of mental health problems, psychosocial interventions, problem-solving techniques, benefits, pharmaceutical drugs and their actions, the Hearing Voices movement, stress vulnerability and its developments, mental illness resolution in other societies,

New Ways of Working,[3] the Mental Health Act.

4. Networking opportunities. This is where you meet others who want to change the system, make constructive use of their painful experiences, and lobby to effect change.

Contributing to local and national movements and committees with my first-hand experience, and influencing policies and politics has proved to be a satisfying and productive activity for me and for other carers. As these also bring me into contact with survivors and those seeking and finding alternative humane ways to help service users move on and regain control over their lives, the experience is absolutely life-affirming.

Carers should be recognised and valued as equal partners alongside paid mental health workers; our comments should be heard and taken seriously, and we should be able to contribute to, and be kept up to date with, care plans and any changes in personnel which may be of relevance. 'Partnership' is often quoted but less often truly observed in practice. Carers need professional support too to maintain their own health, so Carers Assessments should be kept up to date and taken very seriously. The vulnerability of carers, subjected to unrelenting stress in all aspects of their lives, should be evaluated, recognised and properly addressed.

Resources and services that would be helpful to carers[4]

- A full-time carer-link person based in the ward, someone who is there and dedicated specifically to meet, and help the carer or family through those first weeks of admission

3. Information can be found at http://www.newwaysofworking.org.uk
4. This section also appears in Appendix 1 (pp. 115–17) along with all other contributors' helpful learnings and essential information.

trauma, would make a real difference. This person could offer some comfort and introduce the carer (preferably personally) to sources of practical help, people, organisations and literature. They would also be there to help with the later problems that arise on an individual case-by-case basis. Such a person is particularly necessary in the early weeks when the whole family is completely lost and without any support systems. This person should be genuinely interested in carers and families, not someone delegated because no one else wants the job, and probably not a member of the ward staff. The post needs to be properly funded so the person can provide a reliable service.

- A carer's advocate would also be invaluable. Most carers do not know their legal rights, and it is a complex and ever-changing area. A short leaflet geared especially to the new carer should be given to him or her by ward staff on admission of the patient, with details of the named nurse, relevant ward routine, ward phone numbers and those of support services in and outside the ward itself, local and national. A simple introductory empathic humane statement would be very reassuring.

- It would really help to have a neutral person available who can mediate at difficult times.

- Having a carer crisis helpline open on a 24-hour basis seven days a week and a specific family support worker attached to the Community Crisis or Home Treatment Team would make a real difference and could prevent many readmissions to acute wards.

- Literature, advice or, preferably, practical training on 'defusing' techniques for difficult mental, verbal and physical situations would also be useful. Carers are often in dangerous situations alone with no back-up support. This is something professionals rarely have to meet, but carers are left to manage as best they can, sometimes for many days and nights without a break or sleep.

- It is assumed any problem will be about transgression in a specific matter or by an individual rather than a more diffuse cultural or generic concern. There should be a way to address these latter concerns, with the Ombudsman for appeal in dispute. For example:

  - It is assumed that an NHS complaint will be very specific, someone (i.e., a particular person) said or did something unacceptable at a particular time, rather than a general unhelpful, negative, unkind or dismissive attitude manifested by many staff, perhaps everyone in that sector of the service. I see this as a general cultural problem that needs to be tackled.

  - It is difficult for an individual to stand up against a pervading cultural practice, and I know good mental health service workers who have been forced out of the service, or become ill after they have been ostracised by colleagues because that person is seen as 'siding with the carers' or 'whistle-blowing' about malpractice.

Both examples illustrate the 'us' and 'them' situation that is widespread in the NHS. This is *not* partnership.

- I understand a system for monitoring the patient's sensitivity to specific neuroleptic drugs is in use in Scandinavia in order that permanent nervous damage, like loss of speech, various dyskinesias,[5] involuntary movements, excessive salivation, restlessness, lack of concentration etc, can be avoided. It would be good to have this in use here.

5. Difficulty with, uncontrolled, or distorted control of movement.

- Stories of how individuals have achieved recovery are needed to give hope to service users and carers alike (see p. 124).

- The International Society for the Psychological Treatments of the Schizophrenias and other Psychoses (ISPS), the Social Perspectives Network, Hearing Voices Network, Critical Psychiatry Network and the Soteria Network offer discussion, ideas, enlightened research and models that can be copied and extended. They generate hope (see pp. 120–4).

What carers can do for themselves
- Take time out. Being out of doors, gardening, walking in the countryside, by the sea, being with animals, socialising with others – sometimes those who have a similar problem, and at other times, those who are not involved in mental health issues can really help at difficult times.

- Reading is useful. A good book has been my companion through many a sleepless night. Locally, there has been promotion of reading in groups, the book serves as a focus for discussion and has been particularly helpful to people suffering from depression; I have heard this aptly described as 'Prose rather than Prozac'.

- Physical exercise I have found helpful include, Tai Chi, Qi Gung, Pilates, Alexander Technique, Yoga, swimming, walking, etc. I find activities which help build core strengths, affecting both mind and body are particularly useful.

- Learn to say 'No' sometimes, and keep to it.

- Being companionable, learning how to help both yourself and others and offer mutual support towards recovery. A good local support network is crucial, people you value and with whom you are at ease and can be honest, open and yourself, to know that you are valued. A joint project like developing a social enterprise gives practical scope and focus for creativity if that's a genuine interest for several people and someone has a good project idea.

- A related strategy I find most supportive to me is to link with others working for change and influencing the direction, pace and outcome of that change, anywhere in the world. No one should have to travel this difficult path in isolation, and we have much more power if we get together, organise and work in a coordinated way.

Maybe we need to develop a Mental Health Carers' Union.

Chapter 5
A young carer: Jasmeen's story*

Jasmeen

My mum was diagnosed with schizophrenia about a year after I was born. My dad told me she was first diagnosed with post-natal depression, but then they changed their minds. That was 16 years ago. My dad is a dentist and we live in a suburb of a big city, where my dad's practice is about three miles away. I have a brother Sameer, three years older than me, who is now at university.

My life has been completely dominated by my mum, or should I say by my mum's schizophrenia. I haven't wanted to find out too much about it because it's been my dad and Sameer who have dealt with the doctors, social workers and hospitals. I think they have tried to protect me, but at the same time, my life has been taken over by looking after my mum when she is here. Another reason I've not wanted to find out about it is that I was frightened in case I found out that it runs in families and I am going to get it too.

When I was very young, my earliest memories of our house were that it was always complete chaos, dirty and untidy. Because dad had a good job we had a cleaner who came in once a week, but everything was in a state the day after – it didn't last long. My dad was out at work and mum didn't do any cleaning or tidying, she made things worse or sat staring at the wall. Not out of the window, but just

---

* This account is based on interviews with young carers. The names, details and events have been altered, but the issues remain the same.

looking at the wall, with her eyes half closed as if she was trying to make out some detail of a picture, but it was just the wall. That's how I remember her when she was quiet and she still does it a bit, but she is actually much better now. I mean that she doesn't actively do many things, but she doesn't do a lot of what I call 'mad' things either. I used to feel relieved when she was quiet, but when I got a bit older, after an hour or so I would worry about her. I don't worry about her when she's quiet now, as long as I know where she is and she's safe. When she wasn't quiet she would go around shouting in all the rooms in the house, one room after another. That's how I remember it. I was asking Sameer about this just last week and he said that she was OK some of the time, and when she was she would take us to the shops with her, but I can't remember that.

I remember the house was always in a terrible state with stains on the carpet where tea, coffee and orange squash had been spilled, piles of washing up, food left on the table – not on a plate, just on the table. Drawers left open with things out all over the place and the radio on (Mum was always looking for what she called 'evidence' in the drawers and cupboards. Even now it's still a problem every now and then, but I realise that it's nothing to be worried about. I hated it then though, I was ashamed of our house and my mum. Especially since my dad would shout at me when I was quite young, five or six, I think, and tell me it was my job to clean the house and keep it tidy as soon as I got back from school.

I've made it sound really bad, but even though all this was going on at home, I loved my mum and dad and still do. My dad kept on working most of the time, and he was lucky because he was his own boss. One day when I was about six or seven I was in bed going to sleep and I remembered that Mum had only become ill after I was born. So I put two and two together that it must be because of me – that it was my fault my mum was ill. So there and then I thought that since it was my fault, I could only make things right if I looked after her and Dad and do all the housework. So I started tidying things up after her everywhere she went. It was a very practical decision. I just thought, in my childish way, that she might even get better if I was a good girl. I didn't feel guilty then. I started feeling guilty later when my Auntie Ameera came to stay.

From as far back as I can remember, I knew that Mum was ill, but I don't remember when I was first told. I suppose it must have been my dad. I do remember, though, always knowing we weren't normal, like the other families. In the first place, no one else in my street or class had a white mum and an Arab dad. I wasn't allowed to bring friends home and I didn't have friends at all really because all the kids made fun of me and my brother – they said my mum was mad and that I was going to be mad too. Sameer used to get into fights about it, but I just cried and then kept myself to myself and stayed on my own, a bit of a loner.

It seemed that I spent every minute cleaning, tidying and getting meals for everyone. Dad's sister came over from Yemen for two months when I was eight and stayed with us. I think it was to help Dad because our cleaner got pregnant and he couldn't find another one, and since then I found out that things got really on top of him. Sameer and I got really frightened and I told my teacher that everything was going wrong at home. After that someone came round to see us (later I discovered it was a social worker) and Dad went to the doctors to get some tablets for depression. Then Auntie Ameera came to stay. It was quite a good time because not only did she help Mum, she took over most of the housework. She did keep having a go at me though: telling me that it was my duty as a good daughter to look after Sameer and Dad, and that it was a terrible thing that had happened to the family. She said that girls were a lot of trouble even though I was a good girl (I think this is what started me feeling guilty, but it wasn't her fault). She said my mum was a weak English woman who couldn't cope with a family and that my dad should have stayed in Yemen.

I didn't then, and still don't have what I would call a 'normal' life. I still don't have friends, really. I go to College, but only for the shortest time I can get away with before my dad gets suspicious about me bunking off. Although we have a cleaner, I still clean up after Mum – everyday, more or less. She's got a little better in recent years in that she isn't as 'mad mad' as often. Although she disappeared for two days a few years ago and ended up in a police station about twenty miles away. See, I can say that as though it's normal. But it's not normal is it? I don't know anyone else whose mum just disappeared for a couple of days.

If she is ill, she will either stay in bed and sleep or just lie there and do nothing, or she will be up and about rushing around (it seems to depend on her medication). That's the worst for me because I feel that I have to go out with her to keep her safe. She will go up to strangers in the street and shout insults at them. She often thinks they are representatives of the United Nations come to infect us with illnesses. I know it's crazy, but I try to distract her so she doesn't get into trouble, but it doesn't really work. I try to calm things down, say I'm sorry and that she doesn't really mean it. I don't get so embarrassed any more. She relies on me. When she's feeling better, she sometimes tells me that I have saved her life.

My typical day is difficult to describe, since another thing is that everything is unpredictable, but not in a good way. My whole day is centred around Mum. Assuming she hasn't been up all night, I go to check that she's in bed first thing. Then I make sure there's nothing left from the night before like ashtrays or cigarette ends on the table. Mum didn't smoke until she went into hospital for the first time, but now she smokes non-stop. She doesn't eat breakfast, but I get her up for a cup of coffee because she'll spill it in bed if she doesn't get up for it. After college I get straight home and look for her. What happens next depends on where she is and what sort of day she has had. I always make a meal for us all and then we sit in together in the evening, Dad, Mum and me. It's just like being a nurse really. Keeping an eye on her, never off duty, never relaxed. I feel I need to do that, to keep an eye on her all the time. It's not that my dad asks me to do it, I just feel I have to.

Dad suggested I went to see a counsellor at college but I didn't get on with him. He did tell me about the counselling place in town for young people and that's where I got some help. Some people my own age and some volunteers, I think. I can talk to people there and I go once a week in the evening. I do feel I've got a tiny bit of my life back since going there, and I've been able to talk about how I think I might get schizophrenia too, and how guilty I feel about Mum getting it in the first place. I also can tell someone how really angry I get. I get angry with Mum and then feel guilty. If she says something mad, like accusing me of stealing her precious things, it hurts and sometimes she's so cruel that I want to lash back at her. Then I feel guilty. They've been very helpful with things like that. Before, I just sat with it and felt ill, sometimes. Obviously I couldn't tell Dad – he has enough on his plate already with work and Mum and everything. I know he thinks his life has been ruined sometimes. I haven't changed how I think though. I still love my mum and think I'll look after her until she dies. No one else will.

Chapter 6
Is anyone there? Will someone please listen? More questions than answers

Anne Fraser

From the very beginning of Emily becoming ill we had difficulty being heard. In the early days when her behaviour became worrying we went along with the GP's assessment that it was 'her age'. But as time went on it became obvious that this was more than the awkwardness of a teenager.

Em, a gregarious, sweet-natured young woman, had just passed 17 when her behaviour first began to give us cause for concern. Initially, people said she was suffering an extreme case of teenage rebellion. Instinctively, however, we knew that something was seriously wrong – her so-called teenage rebellion wasn't just irritating or even infuriating, it was disturbing and frightening. Other carers I've spoken with since have talked of that same instinctive sense. Services, particularly GPs, who are often the first to be consulted, need to take more notice of this gut reaction. I had been a high school teacher for 17 years and therefore had a good understanding of what to expect from adolescents. This was experience that should have been given more credibility when later I sought help and advice. Instead, as my GP later admitted, I was seen as an overly worried mother.

The year was 2000 and Em was in her first year at a further education college studying for a BTec in Performing Arts, making new friends and, according to her tutors, doing very well – a bright young woman with talent.

Initially, her behaviour seemed 'ordinary' enough, for example, she began to not come home at the agreed time.

Slowly this progressed to staying out hours past the expected time, then led to her staying out all night, uncharacteristically refusing to give warning that she wouldn't be home, or reassure us that she was safe. One time I had to physically prevent her from 'going for a walk' at four o'clock on a cold January morning, wrestling her up the stairs. I began to feel afraid for her safety. Families reporting uncharacteristic behaviour of this sort should be listened to seriously from the outset.

Almost overnight she became aggressive and inexplicably confrontational over simple things. (What time shall we have dinner? Can you get your washing down from your room?) She began demanding large sums of money, becoming enraged when asked why she needed it (I thought she might have a drug problem). She was making shocking, sometimes obscene personal remarks, often in public. My unexpressed thought at the time was 'It's as if she's possessed'. Her behaviour became so unpredictable and distressing that we decided to seek help.

As for many people in this situation, our first port of call was the family GP who thought her behaviour was not particularly unusual. He gave us a self-help directory for counselling services; he didn't think there was anything he could do to help. At first I tried to acknowledge that perhaps I was over-anxious, finding her burgeoning independence difficult to adjust to. I tried to live with this new Emily in our midst, resolving not to react in anger to her rudeness and inconsiderate demands, but over a period of weeks this became increasingly difficult as things went from bad to worse.

She was now showing signs of serious anxiety, expressed as fear of rape and violent assault; for example, she thought men passing her in the street could read her thoughts. In part we attributed this to her boyfriend, who according to neighbours had a history of violent behaviour and harassment. She had recounted to us incidents of his violent behaviour towards her and on one occasion we witnessed such an incident. He was also making obscene telephone calls, his attempts at anonymity thinly veiled. Despite pleas on our part for her to stop seeing him, she found separating from him too painful and so too difficult to sustain – to separate from him meant giving up her social network. We were all seriously stressed and so tempers in the house became frayed.

To those who knew her, Emily was obviously frightened. She was expressing an urgent need to get away from home. We tried in vain to find somewhere for her to retreat to. She was staring at us as if we were strangers, sometimes for prolonged periods, sometimes just staring into mid-air. My father (who had just been given a diagnosis of lung cancer) likened it to her being in a reverie. She was grimacing as if in pain, she seemed not to hear or understand simple questions (would you like a cup of tea?) or requests (can you pass the salt?) taking minutes to respond. There were sudden unexplained bursts of hysterical laughter. She wasn't sleeping and neither was I, as I listened to her pacing in her room at night for hours at a time.

She became excessively withdrawn, spending most of her time on her own in her room or out all night. She dropped out of college and started losing long-term friends who found her behaviour too difficult.

During this period there were three more consultations with the GP over a period of approximately six months. Despite my repeated recounting of these extremes of behaviour, he continued to be unwilling to consider that there was a serious problem. For one consultation Em agreed to see the GP on her own. As she walked into his consulting room I watched her gather herself in preparation, poised and performing. I knew she would present to him as a perfectly ordinary young woman having problems with her overly anxious, overly controlling parents.

Life continued like this for several weeks during which time Em deteriorated by the day. There were two emergency medical calls when she was given sedation. After the second call-out the GP finally referred her to community psychiatric services. We waited another very tense and worrying two weeks for a psychiatric assessment with a community psychiatric nurse (CPN).

I thought a psychiatric assessment would mean an assessment of the situation we were in as a family, that Em would be given help to sort out what was disturbing her, that they would want to talk to us, with her, about her history, her life and the stress she was under. At that time I didn't understand that assessment could mean assessment under the Mental Health Act, which could see her forcibly admitted to a psychiatric hospital. I thought we were there to try and avoid hospital admission, to talk about what was going on.

On the day of the appointment we arrived shaken and distressed. Em had had a violent outburst. She was frightened about the 'assessment', refusing to go and had turned her fear on us.

The assessment turned out to be far from our expectations. The CPN, despite our obvious distress, felt that there was no need for any immediate action. She arranged three appointments for Em to have counselling. At the time I thought 'she'll not turn up for those' and she didn't. Once more we had to try and manage the situation alone.

Inevitably we reached crisis, or perhaps more to the point, Em cracked under its weight when, five weeks later, during an uncontrollable bout of anger and fear, she threatened to kill both her father and herself with a very large and very sharp kitchen knife. Unwilling to take any further risk with her safety or ours, at four o'clock one Tuesday midsummer morning, we called the police who took her into police custody, where finally she was assessed under the Mental Health Act and admitted to psychiatric hospital.

Initially there was some sense of relief – finally she would get the help she needed. Once more we expected that nursing staff would talk with us all about that had been going on in the past few months. At last we could talk about the violence from her boyfriend, that she had an excessive fear of being raped, that she was close to her terminally ill grandfather, and that until recently she had been doing well on her course. Perhaps they would want to know what her upbringing had been like, how she had done at school.

However, we talked about none of these things, because there was no talking. On my first visit to see Em on the ward I spent an hour with her (and half a dozen others) in the patient smoking room watching a television that was bolted onto the wall just below the ceiling – the sound was turned down and there appeared to be no remote control. Unsurprisingly there was little conversation going on.

I went to look for a nurse to speak with. Surely they needed information as soon as possible if they were going to help Em get better? Why weren't they looking to speak with me? And when was I going to talk with the psychiatrist? I was concerned about Em being so dopey from the medication – what was she on, what good was it doing, how long would she be taking it for? Why did she have to be on an adult ward and not under the care of Child and Adolescent Mental Health Services (CAMHS)?

When I eventually found a nurse, she seemed unable or unwilling to answer my most important questions. She wasn't interested in my thoughts about why Em had become so distressed; she didn't know when we would be able to talk with the psychiatrist; she couldn't discuss Em's medication. The only question she would answer was that Em was on the adult ward because CAMHS only worked with young people who were still in school. This woman just didn't want to talk to me; her attitude was one of barely concealed indifference, a woman with much more important things to do than discuss with me the whys and wherefores of my daughter's distress.

At this point I began to feel a sense of despair. Surely this wasn't right. Surely we needed to be talking about why Em, at 17 years old, bright, capable, funny, caring Em, was sat smoking in a room with the television inaudible, where, along with her fellow patients, she was unable to talk about anything to anyone.

I pressed the nurse, careful to check the rising panic that was joining the despair lest I too should be seen as unstable. 'When can we all meet to talk about what happens next?' I asked. The reply, essentially, was to wait for her named nurse to return from holiday. She would be on duty next in three days. I was stunned. Three days?!

There was no attempt to explain, reassure, converse, enquire, empathise, provide tissues. I was left crying on a corridor absorbing alone the awfulness of what was happening.

After months of anxiety, fear, confrontation, worry, aggression, sleepless nights, and finally a desperate cry for help resulting in admission to acute psychiatric care, there was still no one willing to listen.

My next attempt was to try and see the psychiatrist – perhaps he was the person to be talking to. The next day I telephoned to make an appointment. I was told, 'I'm sorry he's not here. Can you phone back in an hour?' Then, 'I'm sorry he's in a meeting. Try again after lunch.' And finally, 'I'm sorry he's just left for his clinic. Try again tomorrow.'

And the same the next day, until eventually, after some angry words, an appointment time was given. We were to see him at the hospital the following day, the day Em's nurse was back from holiday. Logically we should all have met together, and with hindsight I would now insist upon doing so, but I was intimidated by the situation, assumed I knew nothing and they knew everything. Em's named nurse didn't come to talk to us as we waited for the psychiatrist to arrive – once more stood on the corridor of the ward (was there not a visitors' room?). She passed us twice before we realised who she was. When I introduced myself she said hello pleasantly enough but proffered no news on Em. When asked, her reply was so vague as to be useless. 'She's fine.'

'How can anyone be "fine" if they have to be in a psychiatric hospital?' was my silent response.

The psychiatrist was 45 minutes late for our appointment, apologetic and wanted to know: 'Why do you wish to see me?'

Was this a serious question? Did he really not know why we might want to talk with him? He went on, once we had stated the obvious. There wasn't much he could say about Em at this stage.

We asked some questions about what he thought was the matter with her – which was when we were told she was psychotic (at this point 'psychotic' and 'schizophrenia' were not linked in my mind) but he couldn't say much more than that. He then asked if there was a history of serious mental illness in the family and if she'd had any serious illnesses as a child. I managed to mention Em's relationship with her boyfriend and my father's cancer which he noted without comment before saying thank you for coming, thus bringing the meeting to a close. We were with him for no more than fifteen minutes.

Again, with hindsight, I wish I'd had more confidence to push for more information, and insist that he took note of what I thought was important for him to understand, but having a daughter in the midst of a serious psychotic breakdown doesn't inspire confidence. I was in the eye of a storm and beginning to wonder if somehow it was my fault.

Because of my experience as a teacher I was also making assumptions about procedures of information exchange that I was accustomed to in education. The health service style of communication is vastly different – ironic given the intrinsic people-centred nature of working in psychiatric care – talking with people didn't seem to be high on the agenda.

Em was in hospital for three months. In that time I had one conversation with a nurse that I felt helped make sense of her psychosis. He was prepared to consider with me who, figuratively, the magician putting thoughts into her head, might be. This to me was an example of good practice, he gave me hope. He talked with me as an equal who had pertinent contributions for Em's care – there was a genuine exchange of information. Unfortunately we only met the once, after that he moved to another job.

Other than this, communication with ward staff was poor. On one occasion Em's named nurse, in an effort to communicate, explained the theory of High Expressed Emotion (HEE)[1] which only served to increase my growing sense of guilt. On the days when I couldn't face the silent TV and smoking room, I would telephone to ask how she was. Usually I was told to ask Em myself because they couldn't tell me. Sometimes, if I was lucky, I'd be told if she'd had a good day, or if she'd joined in when takeaway food had been ordered for the evening. I made one or two more attempts to

---

1. We acknowledge that among carers this is a controversial issue. It is said by some that when caring for people with experience of psychosis, the carer often becomes upset, which can lead them to direct negative feelings and criticism towards the person they're caring for. This type of behaviour is thought possibly to contribute to the likelihood of relapse for the mental health service user. See, e.g. *Expressed emotion in carers of people with first-episode psychosis* at www.mentalhealthcare.org.uk.

talk with ward staff, but they were fruitless.

For several weeks after admission, Em remained dazed and confused. She was very angry with us. Why had we put her in hospital? Why couldn't she come home? 'Please let me come home, I promise I'll be OK, pleeease.'

Her pleading left me feeling like a traitor. On the drive home I would have to pull over; I couldn't see the road for tears. Surely there was an alternative to the hospital. To see her so unhappy was too painful to ignore so I made enquiries and found an alternative – Beech Grove – a facility for young women with serious mental health problems which required a referral from her psychiatrist.

Again it took days to track him down to discuss the possibilities of a transfer. When we did speak he was obstructive and unwilling to consider any potential benefits it could offer. He doubted the change would make any difference and, despite being asked repeatedly if this was his clinical opinion, he wouldn't give an answer. His only concrete observation was to say, in a tone of accusation, 'You seem very interested in your daughter's care, Mrs Fraser'.

'Of course I am. What else would you expect me to be?' was my reply.

Now it seemed as if I was under the microscope for being determined to help Em. It seemed that my refusal to accept Em's treatment without question was going to be viewed with suspicion and irritation. Em never went to Beech Grove, in the end from her own choice, but in my opinion her choice was an ill-informed one.

And so this went on for the twelve weeks she remained in hospital, where gradually she improved sufficiently to be discharged home. Her improvement, however, was far from a return to the young woman she had been. She was still withdrawn, her confidence at rock bottom, she viewed us with suspicion, conversation was difficult. She was very unhappy about her gain in weight as a result of the neuroleptic medication (firstly Respiridone and later Olanzapine) complaining that it prevented her from 'thinking straight'.

'It's like having cotton wool in my head. How am I supposed to get better on this? I can't think.'

Initially she tried hard to establish a routine. She volunteered briefly at the local Oxfam charity shop. We took on board the HEE hypothesis: that family tension and stress could contribute to relapse; but living with someone trying to recover from a serious psychotic breakdown makes for a lot of tension. She got very cross when I tried giving her advice about her diet to help reduce the weight gain. I wasn't surprised or offended, she was 18 and didn't want her mother's advice – this to me was normal and healthy.

It became clear to me that the family are not appropriate as sole motivators; we cannot help but be too subjective. We are placed in a position of constant vigilance, which in turn creates anxiety. The minutiae of everyday interaction become charged with such great significance that it becomes impossible to relax in each other's company.

I'd been told that I should speak to her CPN if I had any concerns – the same nurse who had said weeks earlier at the psychiatric assessment that there was nothing she could do. I had little confidence – unsurprisingly our communication with her was poor. In part this was due to her heavily accented and poorly spoken English (she was from Finland). I could see Em was finding the necessary concentration to understand her difficult. I tried to discuss Em's concerns, particularly about the medication, seeing myself as an advocate for someone who was still very confused and having serious trouble communicating. I asked about possible alternatives – were there any talking therapies available? Was there anyone she could talk with who had been through a similar experience? (this suggestion had come from Em herself during one of our few conversations but she didn't feel able to ask the CPN herself).

The CPN said she could only discuss these things with Em – because of confidentiality Em had to give her permission for the CPN and I to speak. No amount of my trying to explain Em's state of mind – that she was having serious difficulty forming ideas and reasoned thinking, that ordinary discourse was too demanding – would budge the CPN's position. This was the confidentiality principle, intractable and unyielding. The CPN was unwilling to negotiate a way for us to communicate so that we could work together to help Em get well. For the nine months Em was at home before she was re-admitted to the hospital, I battled constantly with the statutory services for effective communication. Unknown to us at the time, Em had insisted that the care team could not speak with us. We were not made aware of this until after Em was re-admitted. Effectively we were left completely in the dark at a time when absolute clarity and openness were essential if suspicion, miscommunication, and paranoia were to be avoided as far as possible.

Apart from her self-consciousness because of the weight gain, the medication also made her feel tired. She lost motivation – staying in bed, locked in her room – she withdrew and became increasingly depressed. Em was now avoiding the CPN, missing appointments or not answering the door when she called at the house. The CPN would leave a calling card with another appointment date for two or three weeks hence, follow-up never happened within a day or two. Thus her care team were going for weeks without contact and so had little or no knowledge of how she was. I suggested to the CPN that she make appointments or telephone when I was at home. She refused to do either, maintaining that Em had to take responsibility for her own recovery.

I had been reading about mental health problems and by

now I was much more informed about the nature of psychosis and pointed out that her withdrawal was possibly symptomatic of someone still in distress. I could see that Em continued to experience confusing thoughts and ideas. It seemed to me that she was afraid to speak for fear of having to go back into hospital.

She had been out of hospital about three months when her deterioration started to become obvious. From then on there was a continual decline. Weekends became particularly difficult as Em developed a pattern of going out drinking, using cannabis, once more staying out all night without letting us know she was safe. Once or twice she came home in the early hours with unknown young men to sleep overnight. Having strangers in the house under the circumstances felt unsafe and very uncomfortable.

From Sunday afternoon through to Friday afternoon she was a recluse, picking up on Friday night to start again. In the week she was distracted, tired and palpably unhappy. We all were. It was almost impossible to discuss with her the pros and cons of drinking alcohol, cannabis use, lack of sleep and sex with strangers. Trying to talk about these matters usually degenerated into arguments.

Most weeks I would make futile attempts to speak with a member of her care team desperate for them to be aware that her behaviour was becoming increasingly risky and unpredictable, that she was relapsing. We would come home to the front door left wide open and no one in the house; the kitchen filled with gas fumes where the burner hadn't been fully turned off; we had to change the door locks when keys were repeatedly lost. Money slipped through her fingers.

It took eight months before we once again buckled under the weight of this tension. After a particularly difficult weekend Em broke down in a hysterical rage, took all the kitchen knives from the drawer, the medication from the cupboard, locked herself in her room and again threatened to kill herself. When we telephoned the psychiatric hospital they refused to help, saying because she was threatening violence we had to call the police. There was no reasoning with them that the police would make the situation worse. Eventually with all the calm and nerve we could muster we coaxed her from her room and with the help of a much loved friend she was driven to hospital and persuaded to stay 'just for a few days, until you're feeling a bit better'.

A few days became eleven months. That day eight years ago was the last time we saw our lovely Em. Coupled with the continued shield of confidentiality and the services' inability to communicate with us she refused to have any contact believing we had done terrible things to her when she was a small child.

Today we are led to believe via unofficial sources that she is doing as well as can be expected. She is maintained on medication that requires regular monitoring because of the risk to her immune system and heart functioning. She lives in low-supported housing and seems to have made a life for herself. We think that her continued refusal to see us is in part due to needing a reason to explain why she became ill and if that reason helps keep her stable, we live with it, but with a great sense of sadness. We can't help but wonder that if there had been a genuine desire on the part of services to listen and develop a partnership, a dialogue with those of us who knew her the best, that perhaps she would have a reason that is closer to the truth and we would still have contact with her today.

Postscript

Since writing this story Em has made contact, almost eight years to the day since we last saw her. We are of course overjoyed but also overwhelmed. These early days are, in some ways, anxious times as we readjust to one another's company and carefully catch up on all those missed years. I'm so pleased to say that she is the same gregarious, caring and funny girl, now a woman, that she was eight years ago. We hope that this is the beginning of her recovery. She has chosen to come off all medication, believing that this in part is what has motivated her to take the step to contact us. Currently we are waiting to see how she will react to being medication-free as there can be negative consequences to sudden withdrawal. In the meantime we're making the most of having her back amongst us and will take each day as it comes. Wish us luck.

Possible questions for a carers' assessment[2]

Do you feel able to talk with …, X's care coordinator?

If not what would you like to do about it?

How regularly would you like to have contact with X's named nurse/CPN/psychiatrist and in what way?

In what ways can X's nurse/CPN be of support to/work in partnership with you?

What action would you like to take, or for others to take, in the event of signs of relapse?

What help do you want if X goes into a crisis?

What are your feelings regarding medication? Do you think there are other approaches that could help X?

What needs to be done to reduce your anxiety about X?

---

2. This section also appears in Appendix 1 (p. 117–18) along with all other contributors' helpful learnings and essential information.

What information do you need about X's mental health problem?

What information do you feel is important to share?

How would you like to see that information being used?

Do you feel able to care for X? Do you want to stop your caring role?

What is the most difficult thing about being a carer? What could help?

How does your role as a carer impact on your relationship with the person you care for?

What support do you need as a carer?

Would you benefit from mediation?

Would you like to have contact with a carers' support group?

In an ideal world what would you want?

What suits you in terms of the amount of contact with a care support worker?

What type of daytime provision would be good for X?

Chapter 7
Emergent themes and suggestions for improving care

Jen Kilyon and Theresa Smith

These accounts are obviously the contributors' experiences of what happened. Others, such as practitioners, and even at times those experiencing the distress, may have different perceptions of events and what might have helped. However the way that families and friends experience and perceive the psychiatric system has a huge impact on their ability to survive and continue to provide support. Perceptions need to be shared and understood by all before services can claim to be genuinely meeting the needs of service users and carers. This includes the need for carers themselves to be able to recognise and understand the professional views of practitioners and the constraints under which they are operating.

Some of the points raised by the contributors, such as the ignorance and stigma that still surround our understanding of mental distress, are beyond the scope of a book like this. Some of these wider themes will be dealt with in the other books in this series.

Our suggestions of what can be done to improve the situations in which our contributors and many others find themselves are included below. There isn't space here to go into great detail but the additional information in Appendix 2 should enable readers to follow up some of the ideas presented here.

It is interesting to note that none of contributors have suggested that their situation would have been much improved if only they'd been offered a carer's assessment or respite care. These, alongside carer support workers, are the standard mechanisms supposedly put in place by mental health providers – probably because these are centrally imposed targets that have to be met. However, in reality they rarely meet the needs of families and friends or make a significant difference to their lives, as they may not actually address the issues that really matter to carers – the seven main themes we have identified.

Carers' assessments and respite care can even add to feelings of helplessness and make family and friends feel 'done to' rather than worked with – that it is their job to cope, make the best of things and be grateful for the crumbs that services can provide. The kind of support that carers are routinely offered – if they are lucky – rarely allows or encourages carers to challenge the system. For example, when one of us was involved in the process of reviewing the carers' assessment documentation used within one mental health trust, we insisted on inserting the question 'Would you like to be involved in service improvements?' This was changed to 'Would you like to be involved in improving services for carers?' The working group, which included family support workers, couldn't understand the difference.

We've both met many carers around the country and they generally say they want nothing for themselves. They just want their loved one to have access to a service that focuses on hope and recovery and genuinely meets their needs. What carers are asking for is a different mental health system that looks at the individual as a *person* and what they need, rather than concentrating solely on treating their symptoms.

Emergent themes

All of the accounts in this book share a significant degree of frustration with, and criticism of, mental health services but our intention whilst putting this book together has always been that it should serve as some kind of guide and not just a catalogue of disasters where services prove to be inadequate. To conclude, then, we suggest how these stories can be used to point a way forward for families, friends, mental health workers and organisations.

Obviously there will be other issues that family and friends might raise; however, the themes we have identified below are those that occur with the most frequency from the contributors' stories. Although we have separated out these themes they do, of course, overlap. Therefore many of the possible solutions will also be interlinked.

1. Difficulties in identifying early signs

All the family members in this book who are parents described how difficult it can be in the early days to distinguish between, for example, 'typical teenage behaviour' and emotional distress which eventually developed into psychosis.

Liz Swannack Chapter 1 (pp. 9–10) says:

> So when people ask me when my son first became ill I really can't say. ... He changed from being a very thoughtful, sensitive and caring boy to a young man who was difficult to communicate with and didn't appear to want to commit himself to anything – even, for example, when, or whether he'd be back from school. At the time I attributed this to adolescence and a natural desire for independence and privacy.

Georgina in Chapter 2 (p. 29) writes that:

> Initially, the confusion in itself was overwhelming. I was
> plagued by thoughts and questions. Is he just being a
> difficult teenager? I'm sure he's smoking cannabis. ...
> Following 15 months of sheer hell and three visits to his GP
> – I was told twice that I'd have to bring him to the surgery
> in person. How was I expected to do that when my son had
> totally lost sight of reality?

And when, in Chapter 6 (p. 78) Anne Fraser tried to seek
help with Emily:

> As for many people in this situation, our first port of call
> was the family GP who thought her behaviour was not
> particularly unusual.

2. Expectations that services would help solve the problems

It is not an unreasonable expectation that a lay person, a
member of the public with no understanding of mental
health problems or services, should think that mental health
services will help solve the problem, or improve the situation
fairly quickly. It is doubly difficult for them to understand
how a medical service (which mental health and psychiatric
services are) doesn't have the kind of reassuring immediate
impact on distress that other medical services have. As well,
the fact that information about mental health problems, the
rights of service users and family carers, is not *routinely* issued
– as it would be if a patient were attending for other specialist
medical treatment – is even more disorientating and anxiety-
provoking for friends and family caught in a frightening
whirlwind of events.

Liz, Chapter 1 (p. 14) says:

... they recommended a Mental Health Act (MHA) assessment. As someone with a background in education I thought this seemed like a very sensible way forward. If there is a problem, you assess it then draw up a plan to meet those needs and act upon it. We were persuaded that 'this would be for the best' and Joe was admitted under Section 3 of the Mental Health Act.

Anne, Chapter 6 (p. 80):

I thought a psychiatric assessment would mean an assessment of the situation we were in as a family, that Em would be given help to sort out what was disturbing her, that they would want to talk to us, with her, about her history, her life and the stress she was under. At that time I didn't understand that assessment could mean assessment under the Mental Health Act, which could see her forcibly admitted to a psychiatric hospital. I thought we were there to try and avoid hospital admission, to talk about what was going on.

Morgan, Chapter 3 (p. 39):

Our first impressions were quite favourable: the staff were friendly, and there was a pleasant atmosphere.

3. Lack of informed choice about treatment options
Above we highlight the widespread general lack of *basic information* immediately available to patients and carers on first contact with services. Now we turn to the kind of *treatment consultation* relatives, friends and carers might expect from any medical specialist.

In Chapter 1 (p. 11) Liz describes what happened when her son first had an appointment to see a psychiatrist:

> I believe Joe was given a prescription but I didn't know
> what it was for or what effects it could have on him.

Georgina explains in Chapter 2 (p. 30) that when Christian was first prescribed medication there was an equal absence of discussion:

> That was it, nothing more was said. We weren't warned
> about the effects that the drugs would have; for example,
> he started to sleep for 16 hours a day and walked around
> like a zombie with lead boots on.

Morgan, in Chapter 3 (p. 39) describes how other 'day-to-day care' decisions, which nevertheless had huge impact on the patient, were made or rescinded without consultation or warning:

> There was also concern about her ongoing problems with
> eating. However, staff got her some special rye bread (she
> has an allergy to wheat), and with their gentle support and
> encouragement, she started to make herself toast, and eat it
> (she had virtually stopped eating at home). This, for her,
> was significant progress.
>
> The ward manager had been on leave when my wife
> was admitted. When she came back, she immediately
> insisted my wife be given full meals from the standard menu
> (or a vegan variant since my wife is vegan) instead.

And finally, in Chapter 4 (p. 61) Marion Hughes remarks how

> The contrast with the models of shared management,
> education and discussion for cancer and diabetes patients
> and their families, and my recent experience of orthopaedic
> surgery and after-care in the NHS, couldn't be more marked.

4. Staff attitudes

All contributors describe the ways in which staff relate to family members and friends and the person in distress. It is true that in each case we are also given examples of staff who *are* empathic, spend time listening, understanding and acting to make life easier for all concerned. However, based on the experiences of contributors and our own wide experience in discussion with carers, these committed, thoughtful and caring individuals are the rare exceptions. They prove that treating people with empathy and respect are the cornerstones of effective communication and an essential component in recovery.

Morgan, Chapter 3 (pp. 41–2), tells us of the desperate measures he had to make to help and possibly even save his wife's life because of intractable attitudes of staff:

> Because she had self-harmed by cutting herself in the past, they insisted that when she was in bed, her arms must be outside the covers at all times ... My wife has osteoarthritis, which makes it very painful to hold her arms in such an unnatural position. Her arthritis also makes her much more susceptible to cold than most people, adding further to her pain and distress at being forced to do this ... At the suggestion of an independent advocate, who had also visited my wife on that day, and who had been appalled at the brutal, bullying attitude of staff there, I contacted a solicitor who specialised in the mental health field.

Later in Chapter 4 (p. 55) Marion Hughes describes the situation on visiting the ward thus:

> If I tried to talk to ward staff, I met their blank indifference.

And Anne recounts in Chapter 6 (p. 82) when she tried talking with a ward nurse:

This woman just didn't want to talk to me; her attitude was one of barely concealed indifference ...

5. Confidentiality

Information sharing is often complicated by differing interpretations of 'confidentiality' – possibly because of practitioners' fears of breaking their professional codes of practice. The problem seems to lie in understanding how to protect patients' medical information on the one hand, whilst understanding how that information might be shared – with the patient's permission if possible – in the service of their recovery. We note that this difficulty has been referred to before in the literature. Pam Jenkinson, founder of the Wokingham Mind Crisis House, noted:

> There was, for instance, the consultant psychiatrist who tried to undermine our crisis house by criticising our lack of confidentiality ... Our role is not professional. We are *community* care and the community is not confidential. It is based on Mrs Smith meeting Mrs Jones in the High St and telling her that Mr Brown has had a fall and needs someone to get his shopping. It is dependent on knowing how everyone else is.[1]

Unfortunately, in our experience there are times when confidentiality appears be used as a smokescreen in circumstances where communication is proving difficult. At its worst, when misused, it can fuel suspicion, miscommunication and paranoia for everyone.

Anne, Chapter 6 (p. 87):

1. Page 233 (original emphasis) in Jenkinson, P (1999) The duty of community care: The Wokingham MIND crisis house. In C Newnes, G Holmes & C Dunn (eds) *This is Madness: A critical look at psychiatry and the future of mental health services* (pp. 227–40). Ross-on-Wye: PCCS Books.

The CPN said she could only discuss these things with Em – because of confidentiality Em had to give her permission for the CPN and I to speak ... This was the confidentiality principle, intractable and unyielding.

And Marion, Chapter 4 (p. 54):

Professionals think that no situation is too trivial or too serious to breach the sacred barrier of corporate 'confidentiality' ... Of course I do not need, nor do I want, to know every detail about my adult daughter's life – that would be entirely inappropriate – but I need to know enough to be able to help and support her in the best way in a crisis.

6. Guilt and blame

It is very common for family and friends to feel in some way responsible, either directly or indirectly, for a person's distress, and some interpretations of some theories of psychopathology reinforce this. The added dimension of being subject to the Mental Health Act, which can at times place family and friends in a supervisory and monitoring role, only serves to compound this feeling. Unfortunately, we cannot bring any experiences where staff engaged positively (or therapeutically) with family members on the issue of feelings of guilt and blame.

Marion, Chapter 4 (pp. 58–9):

Of course, I can never be certain whether some early critical event in family life might have made a difference. If I'd recognised it and addressed it, perhaps this mental illness might have been avoided.

Liz, Chapter 1 (p. 20):

> I was the main target of his anger and distress. Why did I hate him? How had I allowed people to lock him up? Why did I go around helping others and abandon him?

And in Chapter 6 (p. 85) Anne:

> Her pleading left me feeling like a traitor. On the drive home I would have to pull over; I couldn't see the road for tears.

7. Lack of belief in or understanding of recovery

Whilst we recognise there are some wonderful examples of individuals promoting recovery, working independently and in mental health services around the country, there is little evidence that the majority of practitioners and organisations have either embraced the notion of recovery in their thinking or integrated ideas of hope and optimism and how recovery can be achieved, into everyday working. This is a sad indictment of any medical or health service – that it cannot embrace and promote the recovery of its clients. Rather the norm appears to be to abandon distressed people to mere maintenance of a lifetime of 'illness'.

In Chapter 1 (p. 18) Liz explains:

> When I asked the ward manager if she could see any hope for the future she told me she'd seen all of this so many times before; he was a young lad who needed to face up to his responsibilities and would be back at least another three times before we'd see any progress. I must learn to 'back off and let him live his own life'.

Marion, Chapter 4 (pp. 60–1):

> … a member of staff said, 'Forget about moving on. It will be years, if ever, before you recover.'… How dare anyone destroy hope like that?

Whereas Georgina and Christian eventually had more positive experiences (Chapter 2, p. 37):

> Chris has done more in the past year than he did in the 17 years leading up to it. I believe this is all down to the factors I've described above and also having an excellent personal assistant, who has supported and interacted with him in so many positive ways.

So what can be done about the themes that have come through people's stories? Perhaps the first thing to recognise is that these issues are not just for or about 'carers' – they are for everyone with an interest in better mental health.

We will go through each emerging theme and outline some of the things that can be done by family members themselves, individuals who work in the system and organisations as a whole.

What can carers do?

1. Difficulties in identifying early signs

- Family and friends should trust their own instincts if they notice changes in the person in distress.

- Before contacting the GP, it is worth doing some research to find out if there are any local user-led groups such as Hearing Voices Network (see p. 120). If you can get in contact with others who have experienced similar kinds of distress, you will have an idea of what has helped them and get their thoughts on what local mental health services are like from a 'user' perspective.

- Look on the Internet for both the above information and contacts, but also, if you prefer, for leaflets and literature from bodies like Mind (see p. 123), the Institute of Psychiatry (see p. 120) and the Royal College of Psychiatrists (see p. 123).